I'm Educated...Now What?

How to Choose and Find that First Job Out of College

Fred Cooper

Turning Point Books
Dallas

ISBN # 0-9765793-1-6

Edited by: Lauren Eckert
Cover Design by: Martha Nichols, aMuse Productions

Also, by Fred Cooper, Successful Interviewing: How to Win That Job

Turning Point Books, 2626 Club Meadow, Garland, TX 75043, (800) 333-9414

Dedication

This book is dedicated to my wife, Sarah, who supports me so lovingly in everything I do and to my sons, Andy and Daniel, who were the inspiration for the book.

Acknowledgements

I would like to thank several people who helped me in the development of this project. My sons, Andy and Daniel, provided me with the idea of writing this book. As this was written for people like them, they offered much input and helpful opinion. My daughter-in-law, Michelle, and my daughter-in-law to be, Amy, also made contributions. My colleague Jerry Witt also provided frequent insights, which were quite useful. Jerry Alexander, director of the Hegi Family Career Center at Southern Methodist University, added a great deal of supportive information, especially with respect to career testing. Lynn Guillory and Dene Allred of Employment Transition Ministry Network assisted me with information on the topic of networking. I would also like to thank the world's greatest Editor, Lauren Eckert, for her work in turning a scramble of words into a book, and the cover designer, Martha Nichols for her fine work.

Table of Contents

Introduction

For the past 25 years, I have made my living in Executive and Professional Recruiting. I have worked with companies, large and small, locating hard to find professionals in various types of positions. Since I have worked primarily in the Paint and Coatings Industry, I deal with people in technical fields such as chemists and engineers, sales professionals, and those who work in manufacturing management.

Frequently, I speak with people I cannot place in positions. In an effort to help job seekers in some way, I spend a great deal of time offering strategies they can use in finding work on their own. There are certain types of people who cannot be placed by recruiters. These include:

- People who must transition from one field to another
- People who are over-qualified
- People who are too old to find a job
- People who have placed too many restrictions on their job search
- New graduates who are just getting started in life

A couple of these points may have caused your eyebrows to perk. You probably took note on the statements that refer to older people and younger people (as most college graduates are younger). Ah, you say, companies are not allowed to discriminate based on age considerations. After all, that's the law, isn't it? Yes, that is the law all right, but the reality of life is these obstacles do exist. Instead of complaining, it is wiser to realize and accept the obstacles, while developing strategies to work around them for your benefit.

Particularly, when I speak with older people or new graduates, I recommend certain strategies I think work well in today's job market. This book centers on the strategies that benefit new college graduates.

In the late '80s and '90s, when the economy was really booming and the information age and dotcom economy was thriving, it was never easier for new graduates to find their first jobs. College job fairs had hundreds of prospective employers vying for the best talent they could locate on the college campus. In talking with the career placement offices in colleges in my community, they report the number of companies that attend those campus job fairs has been reduced drastically.

It is also true in almost every industry, companies are consolidating. In the paint and coatings industry, the number of companies listed in the "Paint Redbook," which is the industry listing of manufacturers, has dropped from more than 1500 in 1982 to about 400 today. In some cases, big companies have swallowed the smaller companies. In other cases, big companies have consumed other big companies, and, in a few cases, smaller companies have managed to swallow the big ones. Regardless, the cold fact is as many industries become smaller, good professional jobs are harder to find!

Hopefully, this book will teach you some strategies that will help you find the best possible job for you in this day and time.

Preface

As a person who has been in the job placement field for a quarter century, and as a father of one recent college graduate and another soon following, I speak frequently with young people who are just getting started in life.

Both of my sons are in the same fraternity. I have observed that not only have many of their friends left college without jobs, but also without any inkling of what kind of career they should pursue. This is particularly true of those who have majored in general fields such as business or the liberal arts. They're educated, but they don't have a clue as to what they might do with that education.

There are many books that deal with the subject of career planning. In one sense, most of the books present the same, or very similar, fundamental ideas. What is different is the authors' perspective. Therefore, my outlook is that of one who has spent a quarter century listening to the wants and needs of employers as well as the wants and needs of job seekers. I've made my living by successfully putting candidates together with employers and meeting the needs of both. Other people who counsel and advise people on careers also have excellent experience and interesting perspectives. Yet, they differ because their living does not depend on having success in putting people together. That is, they do not have to make placements to survive!

Moreover, it is my desire to help my sons and their friends and associates, so I have a real sense of urgency to apply my experience to help young people at this crucial time in their lives.

In addition to my own ideas and experience, I have also sought help from people who run college career centers and others who work in this field. They have excellent perspectives, and I am indebted to them for their wisdom and experience in this area.

I hope the information in this concise book will help you find the best career direction for your life, and, further, help you find the best possible employer to help you get started on the journey.

Part I

Finding the Work That's Right for Me

Chapter 1

What Do I Want to Be When I Grow Up?

One of the first things I wanted to be when I was a small boy was an elevator operator. If you are younger than 50, chances are you've never heard of such a job unless you've watched old movies. When I was just a tot, there was no such thing as an automatic elevator. Elevators were operated by people. Those old elevators were very interesting. They had a complicated-looking set of controls, complete with lights, levers and switches. And, there was a big throttle to control the speed! The operator had to have the ability to manually stop the elevator right at the floor level so that people did not trip when they got on or off. He wore a cool uniform. He had to be pretty smart, too. 10 people could get on the elevator and tell the operator what floor they wanted, and it was amazing how he remembered to stop at the desired floors only.

The job was sort of exciting, too. You see, in those days, elevators had expanding metal gates inside the cabs, rather than a solid door, so that skilled elevator operators could see the floor landings and stop the car at precisely the right point. That meant when the car went up and down inside the long shaft, you could feel your knees buckling as the operator accelerated at a high speed when going up, and you could feel your heart go up to your head as he was going down. Also, you could see the floors zipping by, which gave a greater sense of speed. If you were going 10 floors without stopping, it was as exhilarating as a roller coaster ride, even a bit scary! Either direction, up or down, you pulled some "g's."

The job of elevator operator, in the mind of a child, seemed to be on the same level of skill and complexity as the job of airplane pilot. The elevator operator had to have people skills, also. He would greet everyone who walked onto the elevator and it seemed that everybody liked him. At home, I even played "elevator" inside my sliding-door closet.

Now, what was there about that job that was so appealing to my friends and me? There were several factors. It seemed to require great skill and knowledge. It seemed to be a position of power, as the operator was in full control of such a complex and dangerous machine, like the captain of a ship. The uniform even made him look like a captain. It was a very public position in that the operator had contact with many people, all of who were depending on him. Who wouldn't want such an interesting, exciting, high profile job as that!

As I grew older and manually operated elevators were replaced with the automatic, self-serve types, elevator operators were put out of work. Alas, technology took its toll, and they had to retrain for other jobs. But, I still stayed on the lookout for other types of jobs that would hold fascinating challenges. I always kept an eye out for a future job that would be interesting, take advantage of my abilities and satisfy my desire to serve according to my own set of values.

In other words, I had, unknowingly and unwittingly, established four criteria upon which a job decision should be based:

- Interests
- Abilities
- Values
- Skills

Regardless of age, these criteria should always be the final factors on which career decisions are based. You may stay in the same line of work for a lifetime, or you may choose to change careers several times. Each time you make a career decision, it is these factors that should guide you. Let me define and describe them briefly here, then we will develop them in the pages to come.

Interests

Interests are things you like. It's as simple as that. Every person has a unique set of interests. What are those interests? What things do you like the most? You know if you are interested in football, music, politics, or coin collecting. You know your interests by what kinds of books and magazines you read, what kind of TV programs or movies you like, what events you attend, what you do when you walk into a department store, what type of organizations you join in school, the people you most admire, where you choose to go on vacation, and what you choose to do in your spare time.

Interests can be evaluated in a couple of ways. You can write down a list of things you know are of interest to you. Secondly, you can go through lists of various categories and express preferences of one thing over another. There are many tests that will draw out possible areas of interest you may not even have thought of or considered. These will be discussed in the next chapter.

For starters, it would be a good idea to take a sheet of paper and make a list of things that interest you. These would include things like hobbies, religious beliefs and preferences, school subjects, sports, political matters, or any other areas of interest.

In selecting a career you should do something that interests you. You will be spending at least one-third of your waking hours in your career work. To do something that is not interesting to you, even if it pays well, is to waste your life. I was a hospital administrator for the first 12 years of my career (or, you might say it was my first career), and I knew doctors who had lost their interest in medicine. They felt trapped in their work. For the most part, they simply stayed in the field because they had trained so long and, as one doctor said, "It's the only thing I know how to do." I have a friend in his 60s who quit medicine, went to law school and became a lawyer. He graduated from law school at the age of 65 and has been practicing law for more than 10 years. I take my hat off to him. Even at an age when most people retire, he followed his interests and started a new career he loved.

Abilities

Abilities are things you're good at, things you do well. You may be good at baseball, guitar, chess, math, speaking, reading, writing, singing, dancing, and any of 10 thousand things. This can be evaluated in two ways: things you think you're good at and things others think you're good at. There may be a conflict between these two things. If you've ever watched the American Idol auditions on TV, you have seen in very amusing fashion, there is a disparity of opinion between what the many contestants think about their singing ability and what Simon Cowell and his panel think about their singing ability.

Your career should take advantage of your abilities, both natural and acquired. I mentioned that my first career was in hospital administration. A good manager must have certain abilities. After quite a few years, I realized administration was not a good fit for me. Fortunately, I switched careers before I got too bogged down to do anything about it.

If you want to be a lawyer, you should have excellent abilities as a student—a person who reads well. You should also have an ability to use words well, for words are the primary tools of a lawyer. If you do not have these abilities, you would be very ill placed in the legal field. If you are an athlete, you will not go far without a great deal of ability. In addition to ability, you must also develop certain skills which stem from these abilities. That will be discussed in the paragraphs to follow.

Values

Values are the things that are most important to you. Ask yourself what things are most valuable to you. For example, is your family life, your religious or spiritual life, your business life, your bank account, your avocational life or your love life most important to you?

You know what is most valuable by considering what you would be willing to give up for something else. Suppose you had to make a choice between going to a football game or going on a camping trip with friends. On what basis would you make that decision? All other extenuating factors being equal, which one would you pick? You would pick the choice that had the most value to you.

If being close to your family was the factor having the greatest value to you at the time of your decision, it would place limits on the career and job you would consider. In my work, I frequently place paint chemists. Recently, I worked with a chemist who was an avid environmentalist. Because of the value he placed on environmentalism, there were certain paint companies for which he could not or would not work because they produce paints that use volatile organic solvents (VOCs). He will only work on paint products that are water based! His values determined his career direction within a chosen field.

Skills

Abilities are things you are good at. They can be natural or acquired. Skills are those abilities you have developed through training or experience. The term usually refers to arts or trades done by the hands or body, though it can refer to a talent you have developed. For example, a dentist has skills that have been developed through years of training and experience. He may have had a natural manual dexterity, which would be better defined as an ability, but only when that ability has been developed does it become a skill. A writer may have a certain literary aptitude or ability, but it wouldn't be considered a skill until it has been developed. Consider a pianist. My wife had a greater ability to learn the piano than I, but it took years of practice for her to turn her talents into a skill that could be used in a career.

As you choose a career field, you may not yet have the skills you need to do well. Therefore, the choice would be based more on abilities than skills. The skills might be developed as you receive further training. However, if you already have a certain skill, this might be the primary factor in choosing a career. I spoke recently with a man whose daughter is a talented dancer. She was born with this gift. Her journey into dancing started with an ability that placed her above her peers. Additionally, she was interested in dancing and was willing to make the sacrifices required to develop the skills she would need to make a profession of the field she loved.

Other Factors

Family Considerations

There are other factors that may come strongly to bear in considering a career. If your family has been in a certain business for generations, they may want you to carry on the family business. Also, financial needs and the needs of your entire family may actually dictate this is the best thing for you to do.

Yes, I know everyone out there is telling you to "follow your heart," and in many cases, that is the thing to do. However, if your heart does not lead you in a direction that will make you a living, you may be running down a dead-end street. I know many people who have great ability and skill in art. But, if they cannot find a profitable way to use those skills, they would do better to let that love and interest serve them in an avocation.

You may be in a solid career field that has a poor job market. In such a case, you may not be able to follow your interests. You might have to take a second choice in life. Several years ago, when I was a hospital administrator, I started a Social Services department for the hospital. To staff the department, I placed an ad for a qualified social worker. Within three days of placing the ad, I had about thirty resumes on my desk. I learned very quickly that the job market for social workers was greatly over-saturated. Regardless of their desires, most social workers were forced to find a second best career.

If you were fortunate enough to have a family that offers a career opportunity, you would be very wise to consider it. In this world, you must not pass up any built-in advantage. If you are 6 feet 11 inches tall and have athletic ability, you would be foolish not to consider the opportunities in basketball. Very few people are blessed with such natural advantage, and those who do not take advantage are passing up something that could be good and profitable.

Several years ago, I took piano lessons from a college piano teacher who was well connected in the musical circles of New York City. One day, she was listening to a piano competition at the world-famed Julliard Conservatory in New York City. She was sitting with a famous piano teacher from the conservatory—someone who might be called a "kingmaker" in classical music. My teacher related she was amazed at the number of truly world-class musicians she heard. The Julliard professor said, "The sidewalks of Manhattan are filled with truly great pianists, but none of them will ever make it big. There's just no market." My brother-in-law is a Julliard trained pianist who has played with major symphony orchestras. He also told me he stopped playing concerts for the same reason. However, he has made a living through the years as a teacher on the college level.

Plan B Choices

In deciding what career you want to pursue, you must often consider a second choice opportunity. You may not get into medical school, law school, or a prestigious business school. You may not be quite good enough to make it in professional sports. You may have some physical handicap that could prevent you from pursuing a military career. You may have some family responsibilities that prevent you from pursuing a dream. Or, you may be obliged to live in a location where your first career choice is not an option.

Life cannot stop just because your first choice dream did not come true. Most people must, at one point in their lives or other, opt for a second choice. That second choice can also produce a fulfilling life career for you.

Consider the great football player who was a star in junior high. He was the "toast" of the school throughout high school and college. Everything he did since age 10 was geared toward a pro football career. A professional team drafts him. His lifelong hopes are about to come true. Then he is cut right before the start of his first pro season. He ends up on the street with no job skills at all. There are far more people whose lives have been ruined by this shattered dream than there are successful players on the field. If they didn't prepare for a second choice option, they are doomed to failure until they find another option. The sad commentary is many cast-off ball players never recover.

What I Want Out Of A Job

If abilities, interests, values and skills are the factors for determining what career is right for you, what are the factors that attract you to a given career? That is, what do you want out of a job? Even if you are well suited for a career or a particular job, you should probably ask if it offers the rewards you seek. What rewards should you seek? Usually people desire:

- Money
- Security
- Self-Worth
- A Sense of Accomplishment

Money

Most people would like to say that money is not the key factor in selecting a job or career. To admit such a thing would make them look self-centered and uncaring. But, I believe it is true that making a good living is, rightly, a key factor in selecting our work. And, to desire a good living is not wrong.

Security

In addition to a good paycheck, job security is a major factor in selecting a career or job. Quite often, money and security are inversely related to each another. That is, the more you make the less secure the situation, or the higher you rise, the harder the fall. That is, "no pain, no gain." That's why people will opt for a job with less pressure or chance of loss instead of one that offers more financial reward and visible success.

Take, for example, two Ph.D. scientists with similar degrees in biochemistry. One will choose to work for a big pharmaceutical company for a high salary. The other may choose to work for a government agency like the Food and Drug Administration for considerably less money. The higher paid candidate at the drug company will be under considerable pressure to produce a product. If he does not, he will lose his job. The lesser-paid person, working for the federal government, will have maximum job security. The job may be more routine or less exciting, but the chances of being laid off are almost nil.

My son, who graduated recently from college, had a friend who earned a degree in computer science. He was offered one job by a startup, "dotcom" company with a new product idea, which, if successful would offer a.huge, windfall profit. He was also offered a job with a large, well-established networking firm in the computer industry. He opted for the risky job that paid the most, even though the company's chance for success was clearly limited.

Those are the kinds of tradeoffs you must consider in evaluating money and security in any job.

Self-Worth

Another major reward people consider is self-worth. A person is usually identified with what he does for a living. Being a doctor, a lawyer, a scientist, a salesman or an executive gives us a feeling of who we are. Sometimes, that is good. In other instances, a person might sacrifice happiness and fulfillment for a source of identity. This is always a tragedy. Prestige has little value if you are not happy and well-placed in your career.

A Sense of Accomplishment

This is, perhaps, the most important reward any career can offer. A sense of accomplishment can reveal itself in many ways. For example, it can result from helping people. It can come as a result of righting wrongs, solving problems or creating something new and worthwhile, or any combination of those factors.

In deciding on any career or job, you should ask which of these rewards it offers, and which holds for you the greatest value. As you review the options, these things also need to be considered before making final decisions.

Chapter 2

And You Thought Test Taking Was Over When You Graduated!

There are many ways to identify career possibilities that might be right for you. There are some basic common sense evaluations you can do. There are also some more formal ways you can evaluate your aptitudes. We will evaluate both of these approaches.

Let's start with the more formal methods. Every college has a career center staffed with professionals who are qualified to help you find your place in life. There are also independent career counselors in every community who specialize in helping people find their niches in the job market. Usually, these consultants work with people who are in the midst of career changes—people who have either chosen or been forced to make career changes, as opposed to new graduates. Since your college career center is a free service, why not take full advantage of it? One of the things the center offers is testing. This includes testing for personality, aptitudes, preferences, intelligence, etc. You name it; they have a test for it!

Let me say one thing about career centers you should take into consideration. In talking with directors of career centers in about 10 major universities, I have come to the conclusion, based upon their observations of many years, these tests do have their place but are not to be taken too seriously.

There are several reasons why this might be the case. One of the primary reasons why these tests do not always work well with college students and recent graduates is that, not having been in the workplace yet, the preferences they express on these tests may not be tempered with reality. That is to say, they don't yet understand all of the factors involved in different types of work. The director of one major university career center told me recently that college students see glamorous jobs out there and their preferences tend to be directed toward those jobs. For example, he said students see jobs like sports agents and advertising directors as the most desirable things they want to do. They do not realize how difficult it is to get into these fields. After more maturity and experience in the real world, their preferences will be tempered with reality and the results from those tests will be quite different.

Another career center director told me the results can also vary by what time of the day or week the test was taken. Nonetheless, I think these tests can still have their place in directing you toward certain kinds of work.

Perhaps, you're away from college and cannot conveniently work with the people at your career center. Let me introduce you to some interesting tests that can help you evaluate your abilities and preferences.

If you surf the Internet for these kinds of tests, you will find scores of them. Some are good; some are not so good. Some are very expensive, while others are free. The tests I am recommending to you were recommended to me by several college career counselors.

In general, I am hesitant to put much stock in self-administered tests such as these. I believe a test that is administered, evaluated and interpreted to you by a trained professional has much more value. So, use your judgment in determining how much stock you would place on tests like these.

In some cases, there will be a free, limited version you can take quickly. If you feel the results are accurate and helpful, you can opt to take a more complete version of the test for a fee.

Some Interesting Tests

O*NET, the Occupational Informational Network

This is a program sponsored by the U.S. Department of Labor. It is a huge database of employment information that can be used by job seekers and employers. It also has a series of career assessment tools called O*Net Career Exploration Tools, http://www.onetcenter.org/tools.html. There are five basic test instruments:

- O*Net Ability Profiler (paper & pencil, requires professional administration)
- O*Net Interest Profiler (paper & pencil, self or professional administration)
- O*Net Computerized Interest Profiler (computerized, self-administered)

- O*Net Work Importance Locator (paper & pencil, self-administered)
- O*Net Work Importance Profiler (computerized, self-administered)

These tests are tied to the O*Net database which has catalogued over 900 different occupations.

O*Net is a program that has far more implications and usage than simply career evaluation. It is used by employers to describe, compare, and evaluate jobs for relative salary administration. It can be used by employees and job seekers to evaluate various occupational data. The website describes it in this way:

> O*NET is being developed as a timely, easy-to-use resource that supports public and private sector efforts to identify and develop the skills of the American workforce. It provides a common language for defining and describing occupations. Its flexible design also captures rapidly changing job requirements. In addition, O*NET moves occupational information into the technological age.

O*Net can be a difficult site to navigate. When you first look at the site, you may find it to be rather complicated and user-unfriendly. However, before throwing up your hands, try going to the Online Exploration Tools part of the site. There, you can find your way fairly easily.

Self-Directed Search, http://www.self-directed-search.com/

The Self-Directed Search was developed by Dr. John Holland, who is perhaps the best known name in the career development field. Holland's theory states most people can be loosely categorized with respect to six types: Realistic, Investigative, Artistic, Social, Enterprising, and Conventional. The report of the test results will give you a 3-letter code which classifies you according to these basic types. Occupations and work environments are also classified by the same codes. According to the theory of this evaluation instrument, you will be best satisfied if you select a job that has a code that matches your personal category code on the Holland scale. This test costs about $10. Another value of the test is that it gives you an exhaustive list of different occupations you might consider.

Typefocus.com

This is very similar to the Myers-Briggs Type Indicator® that has been used for decades, but the publishers make it clear the tests are not the same. TypeFocus™ Careers generates seven personalized, interactive and easy to use reports. These reports are all based on the wealth of research available on personality types. The reports are categorized as follows:

- Personality Profile
- Work Relationships
- Two-Person Teamwork
- Lifelong Learning
- Career Choice
- Training and Education
- Getting a Job

You can take a "light" version of the test for free. Then, you are able to purchase a one-year license to use the test. It comes with a manual to help you understand and evaluate the results of the test. It claims not to be a psychological test "because the client has the final say as to what personality type actually fits them best." Be sure to read the explanatory material before using this test.

Alessandra.com

This is a series of tests that measures such things as behavioral styles, leadership skills, sales skills, time management skills, team management, listening skills, and writing skills.

The free test is one that evaluates behavioral styles categorizing you as:

- Director
- Thinker
- Relater
- Socializer.

They will send you an e-mail explaining which of these defines and describes you. When I took this test, I felt on several questions it was difficult to come up with answers that completely and accurately define my preferences. Therefore, it clouded my complete confidence in the evaluation. You may or may not feel this way. You can get as deeply involved and take as many tests as you like. On the additional tests, the results for each range from $13 to $50 depending on the amount of detail you wish to see. One big plus is if you are not satisfied with what you receive, there is a complete money-back guarantee.

Chapter 3

What Kinds of Things Do You Like To Do?

Tests can be very informative, but I still prefer some easy, common sense methods of discovering your aptitudes, interests, and abilities. Let's look at some of these.

Identifying Interests

How do you go about identifying your interests in life? Interests can be evaluated in a couple of ways. You can write down a list of things you know are of interest to you. Secondly, you can go through lists of various interest categories and express preferences of one thing over another. There are many tests that will draw out possible areas of interest that you may not even have defined. These will be discussed in the next chapter.

For starters, it would be a good idea to take a sheet of paper and make a list of things that interest you. These would include things like:

- Hobbies,
- Religious beliefs and preferences
- School subjects
- Sports
- Political matters
- Objectives of organizations

Here are some questions you might answer:

- What courses do I most enjoy in school?
- What kinds of TV shows do I watch?
- What kinds of movies do I prefer?
- What kinds of books do I read?
- When I read magazines or newspapers, what kinds of stories do I read?
- When I browse a bookstore or library, what sections do I go to?
- What department do I go to when I am browsing in a department store?
- What sports do I like?
- What kind of entertainment do I spend my money on?
- What clubs or organizations have I chosen to be a part of?
- What do I do when I go on vacation?
- What do I do and where do I go in my free time?
- Which people do I most admire and want to be like?

All of these answers are expressions of your interests.

Finding Your Niche

In selecting the work you want to do for a living, it's important that you do something you're good at, something you enjoy doing, something that challenges you, something that makes you eager to go to work in the morning.

Let me suggest some exercises you can do to help you in this quest. These are different from tests that ask you to select from a list of options. These will require you to think through some things and write them out on paper.

Exercise #1—Projects That Satisfy

In this exercise, I want you to think back in your life to some projects or things you have done that were particularly satisfying. I want you to write a short paper on this project with several points:

1. Name the project—give it a title that summarizes what you did
2. Describe project in a paragraph
3. Analyze (with action verbs) what you did
4. Write out the reasons why this was a satisfying experience

Let me give you a couple of examples from my own life and experience. When I was in college, I majored in chemistry. I was active in our local student chapter of the American Chemical Society and served as vice president during my junior year and president during my senior year. When I was vice president, I was in charge of planning activities for the club. The major activity during the year was an out-of-town field trip to visit some major chemical companies in Houston, Texas. It was my job to plan and coordinate the entire event. Here's how I would go through this exercise.

1. Title of project: Chemical Society Field Trip

2. Description of project: In this project, I first met with the members to determine what kind of chemical companies would be of greatest interest. We decided on four companies, including Exxon and Dow Chemical Company. I contacted the General Managers of those companies, told him of our desires, and established dates for the visit and objectives for what we would

see. I called the contact people in the company and made the specific arrangements for each stop on the trip. I then made the travel arrangements for the entire group, as well as some fun, entertaining things to do on the side, including a trip to the beach. On the trip, I led the way, made the introductions, spoke for the group, solved all the incidental problems involved in this type of trip, and closed out the projects including the thank you notes, bills, etc.

3. Analysis of the project:

   a. <u>Led</u> the planning meeting
   b. <u>Contacted</u> company officials
   c. <u>Planned</u> the travel and the schedule
   d. <u>Coordinated</u> the trip
   e. <u>Solved</u> the incidental problems

4. Reasons why it was satisfying:

   a. I enjoyed being the leader of the project.
   b. I enjoyed contacting and visiting with the executives of the chemical companies.
   c. I enjoyed doing new things I'd never done before.
   d. I enjoyed the response and gratitude of the faculty and students who went on the trip.
   e. I enjoyed the total process of conceiving, planning, coordinating, and completing this project.

Let me give a second example from my own experience. When I got my first apartment, it was unfurnished. I was single at the time and thought it would be fun to build a special piece of furniture. So I built my own dining room table out of rare hardwoods. Let me point out that I had never done anything like this before. I had no experiencing using woodworking tools. Everything about this project was new to me!

1. Title of project: Dining Room Table, Built from Scratch!

2. Description of project: I first conceived in my mind what I wanted to build, including the size and shape of the table. I then drew a design of the table, first a rough design, then a design-to-scale. I selected the type of wood I wanted and located sources for the wood. Since I lived in an apartment and had no workshop, I had to find a place to work and a source of power tools. A friend of mine who lived in a house just one block away had a garage and let me use the space for a workshop. As I lived across the street from Texas Christian University and was taking some part time classes there, I went to the director of the workshop for the art department and received permission to use the tools in the shop after hours. I learned how to use the various woodworking tools by trial and error (with a little help from experienced people). The project involved the precise cutting of various shapes of wood and gluing them together to produce a finished product. I also had to learn how to use the various types of wood finishes to produce a nice finish. The project took six months to complete!

3. Analysis of the project:

    a. <u>Conceived</u> the idea
    b. <u>Designed</u> the table
    c. <u>Sourced</u> and <u>purchased</u> the materials
    d. <u>Arranged</u> for workspace I didn't have

e. <u>Learned</u> to use woodworking tools and finishing materials

f. <u>Built</u> and <u>finished</u> the table

4. Reasons why it was satisfying:

a. I enjoyed it because it was different than my usual routine.

b. I enjoyed it because I learned to do something I'd never done before.

c. I enjoyed it because people told me they didn't think I could do it.

d. I enjoyed it because of the obstacles I had to overcome to do it.

What I learned from these experiences was not that I should be a furniture maker or a travel planner. Instead, I learned I enjoyed projects allowing me to do new and varied things I'd never done before. I especially enjoyed work that involved talking with people.

Try this exercise for yourself. Consider three or four things you have done that were particularly satisfying for you. Describe them as I have suggested and see what conclusions you reach about yourself.

Considering Work You Have Observed in Life

Another way to discover the kind of work you would like to do is observe the work that others do. You have been doing this all your life. You have done this in real life and you have done it in the world of media.

I was born right after World War II. It was the first year of the "baby boom" generation, that huge population explosion that occurred when the soldiers came home from the largest war in the history of the world. Ours was the first generation to have television. Television opened up a window to the world unlike any previous generation had experienced. For several hours a day, we were able to watch people in every kind of occupation do their work. We were able to form opinions about those kinds of work and decide if we could see ourselves in those situations.

Oh, yes, our parents' generation had movies. However, a movie was, at best, a once a week affair. The exposure was not nearly as intense. They also had books to read, which introduced them to different people in different occupations. But, not everyone was an avid reader. For the most part, the pre World War II generation was limited in their observations to things they could see in the local world in which they lived. Ergo, a child raised on a farm, had a certain scope of vision with respect to occupations. A child raised in New York City had quite another scope of vision. That's a main reason why in the past it was so much more usual to see children do the same thing in life their parents did.

When I was growing up, young boys wanted to be policemen and firemen. They saw people like that in the cities and towns where they were raised. They wanted to be doctors or storekeepers because they all went to doctors' offices and various stores and could see what those types of people did. I never heard a small boy say he wanted to be a stock analyst or a purchasing agent. They never observed anything like that unless their father or uncle did something of that nature.

Young girls in those days wanted to be nurses, teachers, models, or mothers. That's what they knew. That's what they saw. That's what was expected back then.

Times have changed. Everyday you see people on TV working in every profession and occupation, and you form opinions based upon what you see.

A word of warning here: most of the time, what you see on the surface is not the same as what goes on in real life. One of the most popular shows when I was a boy was a program called, "The Untouchables." It was an "FBI v. Mafia" show about the life of a famous FBI agent named Elliot Ness. It appeared he had the most exciting job in the world. He was sort of a real life James Bond. He was involved in all types of behind the scenes intrigue as well as "on the street" action. He was the brains behind the operation, and the guy who wielded the machine gun on the front lines in the dark streets of Chicago. And every week, he was involved in a whole new and evermore exciting case than the previous week! Oh, what an exciting life!

The real world of an FBI agent is far less glamorous. Such a person may be involved in one exciting case in a whole year. You don't see the countless hours, and even days, they spend in stakeouts watching and waiting for something to happen. You don't see the mountains of paperwork they have to produce and sort through. The typical agent is not involved in daily shootouts with bad guys.

That is also true in almost every profession. What you see on the surface is different than what you see in real life. My nephew is a Ph.D. microbiologist involved in cutting edge research at Harvard University. You may read an article in a magazine, or, in rare cases, see a news report on the kind of research he does. What you don't see are the hours and hours and hours of routine trial and error testing and proving he does every day. There are years of tedious work that go into a little 45-second news clip that describes the end result of the research. And, for every story you hear, there are hundreds of stories of projects people slave over that never get told. Even worse, there are some projects people pursue for years with no positive results at all! Yet, if you choose that profession, it is the real, everyday work that will occupy the days of your life.

So, why not make a little more formal study of your own personal observations of occupations. Consider these types of experiences:

- Your actual experience
- The experience of your parents and relatives
- The experience of your parents' friends
- The experience of your friends' parents
- The experience of your professors and their colleagues
- The experience of people in places you have worked
- The experience you see in places where you go for business or entertainment
- Jobs you see on TV or movies
- Jobs you read about in newspapers, magazines and books

If you will document these things, you will come up with a much better evaluation than if you simply think about them.

Make and keep a log of occupations with the following information for each job. You can develop this log over several days, weeks, or even months.

Observe the following about each job:

- Job title
- Job functions
- Everyday duties of that job, as you see it
- Things that seem appealing to you (the upside)
- Things that might seem boring or routine to you (the downside)
- Qualifications needed for that job, as you see it
- What you would have to do to get into that profession

Again, you can work on that log for several days or several months. Then, after you've put it all together, sit down with your parents or a friend or adviser and review the list. See what you think, and what they think. When you narrow the list down to some occupations that seem right for you, start networking. Networking will help you prove whether or not your preconceptions based on your observations were correct. Also, the process could easily produce your very first career job.

Considering Your Own Job Experience

In all aspects of life, nothing takes the place of personal experience. That is also very true as you consider your view of the world of careers. Every experience, no matter how small or menial, will be an important part of your future.

Yesterday I was talking with a man who is a general manager of a paint manufacturing company. He started in the paint industry sweeping the floor of a paint plant. That job led to a routine job on the production floor, which led to a job as a color matcher, which led up the line to a sales position, and so forth. The point is that he started as a janitor and saw opportunity right where he was utilzing the experience he had.

I heard the story recently of another person who went to a farmers market and bought several bushels of fruit. He set up a roadside stand near where he lived and sold the fruit for twice what he paid for it, which was still cheaper than the price at the grocery store. That led him to buy an old truck, which enabled him to start a business that became prosperous as the years advanced. He started with whatever opportunity and experience he had at the beginning and built upon it.

What about you? What jobs have you held? What experiences did you gain in those jobs? Did you take the time to look at the jobs above you in that situation? My first job was sacking groceries for a large grocery store that was part of a large chain. I could see all the occupations that were available in the grocery store. There were some trades I observed in the meat shop, the bakery, and the flower shop. I observed the work of the store manager, who was making a big salary. He was always watching the boys in the store, and, on occasion, he asked some of them if they would be interested in pursuing a management training career with the company.

In addition to the career options I observed, I could also see careers of people who called on the store. There were salesmen who represented the vendors. There were contractors of various types who did work for the store. I could observe the work they did and visualize what careers might spring forth from their work. For example, I could see what the Coca Cola salesman did when he came to the store. Maybe I didn't want to be a Coke salesman, but the careers available in the Coca Cola Company are unlimited.

Have you worked in a department store, a restaurant, a hospital, an automobile repair shop or a manufacturing plant? Have you done any kind of work in the construction or building trades? Look around and see what the bosses do for a living. Would you like to do what they do? What about the world of education in which you have been immersed all your life? Would you like to teach or coach or do anything related to the running of a school?

Perhaps you've never really looked around your own world of work in an analytical manner. Maybe you've never evaluated the possibilities that are right before your eyes! What about the jobs you've had on campus? It's certainly not too late to go back and evaluate the potential that was before you.

Again, take the log we discussed in the last section. List and evaluate the careers you saw. If you worked in a manufacturing plant, there may have been a staff of scientists, engineers or designers, who did interesting work. There were people in accounting and finance. There was a sales organization. Look at all the jobs and evaluate them on your job log. Then, start networking with those people. What could be easier than to go to people who work where you work to learn what they do? That's also true of places you have worked in the past. Get off your posterior! Get away from that computer cocoon! Go and talk to the people you know or the people you knew who are doing things you might like to do!

Considering The Things You Dream About

Now let's look in a realm that's a little different than the everyday world in which you live. Let's look at your dream world. When I was a boy, there was a popular show on TV called "The Millionaire." (That was back in the days when a million dollars was a whole lot of money). On this show, a wealthy billionaire (pretty rare then) had a peculiar hobby. He would select people in various circumstances of life and send them a check for $1 million. He observed what they did with the money, and how that changed and affected their lives.

Today we have reality shows kind of like that. Then, even more realistically, we have lottery winners. Many people have observed their fortunes and fates and made quite a study of that.

What if you received enough money to support you in fine style for the rest of your life? What would you do? To what kind of work would you devote your life? There are some people who would do nothing. I won't deal with that at all. For one thing, that kind of person would probably not be reading this book anyway!

Life would be rather dull and negative if you had to spend your days merely passing away the time. Even if you lived in a palace, it would be a miserable life. So, take a little time and do a little bit of dreaming. Make a list of some things you might like to do. Go back to those things you thought about in the previous sections of this book—the things your relatives, friends, or TV heroes do. Maybe you should even think beyond those practical things you might consider to be in your range of opportunity. Think about them. Write them down.

Consider the story of William Borden, the heir to the Borden's Milk fortune, who once did this. He could have done anything he wanted to do. He was man of strong Christian faith. Upon graduation from high school in 1904, his family gave him a trip around the world. Seeing all the hurt and need of the world's people, he decided to leave the posh life of his family and become a Christian missionary. He graduated from Yale University and Princeton Seminary, intending to go and do ministry work among the Muslims of China. Seeking additional training in Arabic, he went first to Egypt to study. There, he contracted spinal meningitis and died within a month. When they gathered his belongings, they found these words written in the back of his Bible—"No Reserves, No Retreats, No Regrets."

Though his life was short, he spent it doing what he wanted to do. He was a person who was able to follow a dream, even though the dream did not extend over many years. If you have a dream and the opportunity to pursue it, by all means, do it!

Most people do not have such an opportunity. For various reasons including family circumstances, scholastic ability, physical ability or economic obstacles, they must choose something a bit more practical. That will probably be the case for you. Maybe you dream of being president. Though it is possible to rise from nothing and achieve that dream as people as people like Nixon, Reagan, Carter and Clinton have done, there are hundreds of thousands of others who were never able to reach that dream. However, there are plenty of other opportunities that can provide any practical person a lifetime of satisfaction.

If you want to pursue an **impossible dream**, be sure to first purse a **possible dream,** which can lead in that direction if your fortune should so dictate. But don't follow a path that will leave you in the cold if the impossible does not work out.

Consider once again the young athlete we previously discussed. He never graduated from college, nor did he realistically pursue a degree. He merely took enough easy classes to keep him qualified for his football scholarship. How much better to have pursued an education degree that could have landed him a coaching position, where, at least, he could have pursued another career path in the sport he loved.

A young lady, a friend of our family, has a dream of becoming an astronaut. She is pursuing a degree in math and physics. She realizes the possibility of becoming an astronaut is highly unlikely. However, the possibility of a teaching or research career in physics is a very realistic goal. So, she is pursuing that goal, and, if she should be so fortunate, she could even reach her impossible dream. But, she won't find herself in the cold if she does not get there. Regardless, she will still have a wonderful and satisfying career.

If you go to an expensive school, you probably know some students who are already in a financial situation where they could do anything they want. Some of them have inherited large fortunes that are already producing income. They are often known as "trust babies." Some may be the sons and daughters of famous people or wealthy families. In some cases, they will be in the unenviable position of going into a family business, which they really don't care about (It's unenviable if that's not really what they want to do in life).

My parents once knew a family that owned an enormous department store, one of the most famous and best known stores in the entire South. They had only one daughter (the one my mother knew). There was another family in the city that owned a very prosperous bank. They had only one son, a brilliant young man who wanted to become a doctor. He graduated from college, went to medical school and achieved that goal. He was a friend of my father.

As was the custom in high society in those days, the two families wanted their children to marry someone in their "own social circles." Under some pressure, the two young people married. The young doctor never really got to practice medicine, as he was soon called upon to take over and manage the family's fortune and banking enterprise. He was in the unenviable spot of one who had a dream, but could not pursue it. They were wealthy, but were never happy. In addition, they were childless, and the family dynasty ended when they died.

My mother-in-law always said she felt sorry for Prince Charles because he could not truly do whatever he wanted in life, as he was forced to carry the torch for the British royal family.

So, if you have a dream—identify that dream. Determine if it is a practical one for you to pursue. If it is an impossible dream, you can, at least, pursue it in a possible and practical way.

Determining your Interests—the Bookstore Approach

Another way to determine your areas of interest is to think about what you do when you go to a bookstore or library. What section do you go to? To what kinds of books are you closely drawn?

Utilize The Resources of Your School

The Career Center

There are two primary ways to utilize the resources of your college or university. The first is to go to your academic adviser or key professor within your major department. The second is to go to the career center on campus. I recently read an astounding statistic that only 20 percent of college students utilize the campus career center, which is a free resource with tremendous services. In this life, where very little is free, it is incredible so many students would pass up such a helpful and professional group of people who are there waiting to help! Maybe the fact it is free is detrimental to the career center. Perhaps if they charged an extra $1,000 for their services, it would make the center more attractive to the students!

Your Adviser

Faculty members within your department have a good idea which career options would work well for you, and they know you personally. Additionally, they are, or should be, on the top of your networking list. (We will cover networking in a separate chapter). They know people in the institutions and industries who dispense jobs. They have contacts! You should go to several of your professors and solicit their counsel and advice.

Let me say, parenthetically, if you have not established relationships with your professors, you have really dropped the ball in terms of your networking strategies. It has been my observation that in large universities, especially where classes are large and professor contact is more limited, students do not get to know their professors. BIG MISTAKE.

In my experience, it's not difficult to get to know most professors. For the most part, they enjoy getting to know students who are interested in them. Unfortunately, most students view the professor more as an adversary, who stands between them and a good grade, than a friend, who has a capacity to help them. Also, many students are so busy with campus social pursuits, extracurricular activities or part time jobs, they don't take the time to even meet their teachers, much less get to know them.

If you are still in school and realize you have failed to get to know your teachers, it's time to do an "about face" and cultivate them. It's not hard! There's not much competition in the "get to know your professor" club. You'd be surprised how easy it is to do. One way to do this is to ask lots of questions regarding their lectures—questions that indicate an interest in the subject matter, not simply the "How do I get you to raise my grade?" kind of questions. They're so irritated with the vast majority of students who are there only to get credit for the class that when a student shows sincere interest in the course material, they will help in many ways.

If you are out of college, and failed to get to know your professors, it would be a good idea to retrace your steps, go back and find your professors, thank them for the contributions they have made, and seek their advice and counsel. Again, you will find that very few students ever do this. It would be safe to say it almost never happens! You won't be standing in a long line with respect to such a task. Ask them questions. Treat them as the experts they are. Show some respect! It's never too late to develop a partner for your future.

My father was a physician. When he was in his internship in San Francisco in 1929, the physician in charge of the program was very unpopular with the interns. To be frank, everybody thought he was an arrogant SOB. They hated him! My father didn't like him any better than his peers, but made the decision to cultivate him anyway. This man was instrumental in helping my dad with opportunities in his future. In fact, I called the man forty years later when I was on a trip to San Francisco, and he was gracious and helpful to me, too.

Ask your professors to recommend the career options they think would be right for you. Ask them for contacts in companies. Ask them to make contacts for you. They take great pride in making their students successful. They like to know they had a part in their success.

Basic Job Screening Factors

If you seek to find the basic type of work you like, let me give you some major factors to consider. Unlike many kinds of tests where you find it difficult to choose between options, these choices should be obvious to you.

As you evaluate the work of others from the point of view of a college student, it is quite normal to look up to people who are in management positions—people who are big bosses, those who are guiding the destinies of organizations. Our society tells us that to be successful, you must become one of them.

I am a good example of this. Had I evaluated myself with these simple questions in candid fashion, I might have realized that I would have fit better in a field other than my first career. I got out of administration after 12 years and have been much happier in executive recruiting. It has fit my personality and preferences much better.

Consider the first question, "Do you like being a boss or do you prefer working under a good boss?" Most people would answer "yes" to that "being the boss" preference almost automatically. Bosses make more money. They have more prestige. But most people, particularly young people coming out of college do not understand the negative side of being a boss.

Several years ago, I was talking with a salesman for a large paint company, who had been promoted to sales manager, the job every salesman desires when he starts in sales. Who wouldn't want to have their boss's job? After a couple of years, he made the decision to step down from the manager's job and return to his position as a territorial salesman. I asked him, "Why would you do a thing like that?" He pointed out that being a good salesman is very different than being a good manager.

A manager must be a person who often says, "no" to people, a person who takes unpopular stands, and makes other people unhappy as a result of decisions. A salesman is a "yes" person who wants to be popular and wants to make everyone happy. Also, as the boss, he had to deal with the personal problems of those under him. He found it to be an unpleasant and unpopular position. He felt relieved to be able to return to his old job.

Many an entrepreneur has come to ruin when forced into a management role. After inventing a great, new product, he became the head of the organization that produced the product. While he had everything required of an entrepreneur, he had none of the traits needed to run the enterprise.

If you can come to a good, honest understanding of your personality type early in your career and pursue jobs that take advantage of that, you will save yourself many years of disappointment and misery.

Chapter 4

So What Did I Learn From My College Experience?

Consider Your College Major

When you went to college, you may have known what you wanted to major in and what you wanted to do even before you started. In fact, you may have known what you wanted to major in since the sixth grade. Or, you may have kept your options open and selected a major during your junior year. Regardless, there had to be a reason why you selected your major. Go back to the time you made your decision. Ask yourself, "Why did I make that choice? Why did I choose that over everything else?" Were you doing what your parents wanted you to do? Did your larger family influence you in any way? Was it based on something you became interested in during your high school years? Was there a teacher, a friend, or perhaps some hero in your life whom you wanted to emulate?

Was the decision based on a very intense interest in your life? Was it based on some obvious interest, ability, value, or skill?

A Decision Based Upon Interest

I grew up in the days before personal computers. When I was in college, only large corporations and major universities had computers, which were huge, extremely expensive devices.

My university didn't even have one when I started classes as a freshman. I have one friend who was interested in computers from the very beginning of the PC era. He learned everything about the technology. That interest dictated a total change in plans right after he graduated from college, as that was when the PC phenomenon began.

A Decision Based Upon Values

Another friend whom I knew since age 10 or 12 knew he wanted to be a minister. Of all the things he valued in life, his faith was absolutely number one. People recognized his gifts in this direction even from a young age and encouraged him. That sense of value directed what his undergraduate major, his postgraduate major, and every other choice in life would be.

A Decision Based Upon Skills

Another young man had extraordinary talent in baseball ever since he played in Little League. As he grew older, his talent shone brighter each year. That particular ability became a finely honed skill. He was not only the MVP of his college baseball team, but also the entire college baseball conference. That skill directed his choice to select baseball as a career.

A Decision Based Upon Abilities

My sister and my wife both had extraordinary talent in piano all their young lives. They each majored in music. Their choice was truly dictated by their ability. During their college years and beyond, that ability increased each year and directed their choices of careers.

What about you? Was your college major directed by one of those four factors? Here is a set of questions you should ask of yourself.

- What motivated me to select my college major?
- Am I glad I selected that major, or have I had second thoughts about it?
- Is there another field of endeavor that has taken over my interest during college?
- If so, what happened that caused me to lose interest in the field of my major?

As you evaluate the answers to these questions, there are two logical conclusions:

1. You made the right choice
2. You now feel you should change directions

If you feel you made the right choice, you should certainly forge ahead in the direction you have been planning and proceed to find a career in the field of your major.

If you feel you made the wrong choice, you should ask yourself if you need to continue your education and pursue a new and different major—perhaps on the graduate level—or ask if your degree would be sufficient to qualify you for a career in a different field.

My oldest son began with a major in computer science and quickly learned he did not want to sit in front of a computer screen writing code for the rest of his life. Therefore, he changed his major to management information systems, a more people-oriented field. He has friends who continued their majors in computer science and decided in their senior years they, also, did not want to sit behind a screen. It was too late for them to change their majors, but it was not too late for them to change their career choices. Indeed, their computer science degrees will help them in almost any field!

Both of my sons have friends who will receive their degrees in engineering, but decided along the way they didn't want to be engineers. Their degrees, however, will still qualify them for positions in business, where their engineering knowledge will be a real plus for them.

A student who majored in liberal arts, however, would have a hard time going into an engineering or computer related field, unless he pursued additional training in the new field of choice.

Perhaps you majored in humanities or liberal arts and do not feel you can find a good job in such careers. You will be starting your career search from square one. And, yes, you may have to go back and take some additional course work in order to find a job in another field. However, before you make that decision to spend more time and money in a different degree field, you would be wise to look at the wide range of options that probably would not require more academic education.

For example, you may have majored in psychology but don't see a good future in that field, unless you go for a Ph.D. Suppose you have an opportunity to go into real estate. You really don't have to go back and study business. You can go to work for a real estate company and take the professional licensing courses required to get started in the business. You'll gain all the knowledge you need, while gaining real world experience in real estate. A person who majored in business or marketing would have to take the same real estate licensing courses and might not do any better in the real estate field with a business-oriented degree! In fact, there are plenty of successful people in real estate who have no degrees at all!

Evaluating Your College Experience

Let us assume, at this point, that you are going to continue in the field of your major. Here are some ideas for identifying some specific career direction based upon your college experiences.

Your Academic Experience

One very good indicator of how you would best function in your career is how you functioned in college. Obviously, as you pursued the academic work in your major subject, you were required to complete various types of projects.

If you majored in accounting, you were required in your coursework to evaluate financial statements and accounting systems and prepare every kind of financial report or statement. You were required to do auditing projects. You probably designed and set up both manual and computerized accounting systems.

If you majored in chemistry, as I did, you have had a great deal of experience in many types of chemistry projects. You have spent countless hours in organic, analytical, and physical chemistry labs. You have analyzed, synthesized, and crystallized things. You have done formulations, calculations and prognostications.

If you majored in journalism, you have doubtlessly worked on the staff of the school paper. You have interviewed, researched, written, photographed, designed, composed, and distributed. You have studied composition, advertising, photography, sales, computer graphics, and a magnitude of other things.

Did you enjoy these projects? Or, do you think you might have made a mistake in picking your major? Could you see yourself in a job doing this full time? Could you see yourself doing this kind of work for the rest of your life?

The QUESTION is this—based upon your academic pursuits, do you want to continue in the field of your major for your career? Most of you will probably say, "Yes" (I have read research saying in five years, 80 percent of you will be working outside the field of your major). However, at this point, you will probably want to start your first job in the field of your major. Remember, your major does not absolutely determine your occupation. There are still myriads of possibilities!

Your Extracurricular Activities

In college, many students see their academic work as a necessary, but unpleasant chore! What they really love is the other stuff. It's not supposed to be that way, but, hey, that's the culture with which we live.

Boys major in "girls." Girls major in "boys." They all spend more time in the gym than they do in the library (with the resources available on the Internet, many students today hardly know where the university library is located)! Planning the social or club events occupies more of their time than key research papers. Activist types spend more time in their respective causes than they do in their classes! Some students even spend the major portion of their time playing video games.

Even though that's not how it's supposed to be, there's a great deal to be learned from these experiences that will help guide you in your choice of career.

Your choice of major could be a random choice you made, or it may have been determined by your parents or by some childhood pipe dream. **Your choice of campus activities is something you totally decided for yourself.** Therefore, you should evaluate what you do in these kinds of activities, why you spend the time in them that you do, and why you like them so much.

Here's an exercise that will help you evaluate the extracurricular part of your life. On a sheet of paper, list three extracurricular activities that occupy most of your time (if there are three). For each one, first note what type of activity this is. It could be:

- Social
- Athletic
- Academic
- Professional
- Religious
- Social Activism
- Political
- Campus or Community Service

Secondly, list your functions or roles in these groups or activities. You may have had several functions in a single organization over four years in college. For example, in the Chemical Society, I was secretary/treasurer during my sophomore year, vice president during my junior year and president my senior year.

Thirdly, describe exactly what you did in each of those functions. Consider the job description for that office or function and note what you actually did. For example, if you were the treasurer, you collected the dues, prepared the income report, did the accounting and the banking. Was this enjoyable to you, or was it a real drag? The answer to these questions will help you determine what kinds of things you might like to do in life.

Fourthly, determine which of the jobs you liked best and why. Unusually enough, as I look back on the example of the Chemical Society, I liked the job of vice president better than the job of president. When I was vice president, I was responsible for the programs at the meetings. I arranged for the speakers. I worked with those speakers. I arranged for the field trips. I gave the reports at the meetings. I enjoyed the actual work. When I was president, I simply moderated the meetings. I called on other people to give the reports.

It's kind of like an evening newscast. The news anchor will be reporting on about seven to 10 stories. He will introduce the story and then call on a reporter in the field to tell the story. Now, the reporter is the one who does all the researching, interviewing, and composing the news packages. The reporter in the field is the one who gets to tell the story. The anchor is simply reading a script off the teleprompter machine. Yet, it is the anchor who gets all the glory!

Everybody thinks they want to be the "big boss" in life. They are convinced the big boss is the one who has all the fun and the glory. That's really not true! In any large organization, the big boss is not really in control. It's the people under the big boss who are truly in control. Yes, the boss gets the glory, but he is dependent upon those who work under him.

Consider a big political campaign—the presidential campaign, for example. The candidate is the center of attention. The candidate is the one who gives the speeches and shines for the cameras. But, the candidate's time is totally occupied with getting from one stump speech to another. Every stump has a different audience and requires a different speech. And, make no mistake about it, a presidential candidate does not merely speak "off the cuff" to audiences.

Every speech is carefully crafted to give a specific message to the audience and to the local and national press corps that is covering that event. Even what he wears is carefully measured. The candidate does not simply reach into his closet and grab a shirt or tie. That is determined for him. It is the speechwriters, the event directors, and the people behind the scenes who do all the work and determine how well the candidate looks to the public. Ultimately, it is they who determine whether he wins or loses!

Maybe the work you did in those college organizations to support the people in charge was more satisfying than the "top" job. If so, take careful note. A big boss position may not be the most desirable goal. Oh, yes, did I neglect to say that when all does not go well, the big boss is the one who takes the nose-dive!

So consider what you did in extracurricular activities very carefully. That will give you a clue as to what you would enjoy doing in life.

Chapter 5

Where Am I Strong... Where Am I Weak?

Your Opinion

The work you do in life should take advantage of your strengths and weaknesses. In this exercise, take a sheet of paper, draw a line down the middle, label the column on the left, "Strengths," and the column on the right, "Weaknesses." Be honest, even brutal, with yourself as you list these points. If you are a procrastinator, put it down. If you have a short temper, list it. If you are a good speaker, list that. If you meet people easily, that goes on the list! The list should include:

- Character traits
- Habits (bad and good)
- Talents and abilities
- Things you are good at
- Things you are bad at

Remember, this is not to be an exhaustive self-psychological evaluation. This is just a simple exercise of writing down things that come to mind quickly on both sides of the page.

The Opinions of Others

After you have done this yourself, you should find out what other people consider to be your strengths and weaknesses. Go to people you know and trust—people who would be willing to invest a little time in helping you with some frank and honest information. These might include friends, co-workers, former or current bosses, professors, pastors, or other authority figures. Give them a "strengths/weaknesses" page like the one you made for yourself and ask them to complete it for you. It's not something that will take a long time. You're not asking them to fill out a long checklist or complete a survey. You're simply asking them to list what quickly comes to mind. Some may go heavier on the "strengths" side of the list while others may concentrate on the "weaknesses." It doesn't matter. It need not take any longer than 10 minutes. What you want to know is what other people think of your strengths and weaknesses. Usually, they will be quite honest with you if you ask. Try to find at least three people to help you with this exercise.

In my own life and experience, when I was a hospital administrator, I was truly in the wrong type of profession based upon my strengths and weaknesses. I once talked with my boss about this, and he was very helpful in identifying what he considered to be my strong and weak points. It was his evaluation, based on my strengths and weaknesses, that I would be happier in a field other than management. In such case, I would be in a position to help people rather than work in the adversarial, confrontational role of refereeing problems between competing people and groups.

It was to be three years before I actually made such a change. I can now tell you that he was right in his evaluation. You may say, "Well, it's nice that you had such a friendly relationship with your boss, that you could speak so frankly with him in that way." I tell you that was not the case—that my boss and I did not have a smooth relationship. However, even in situations like that, it's uncanny how an adversarial person can help you.

Through the years, I have found that to be true when I have obtained references on candidates who did not get along with previous bosses. Even though they did not like each other, they were honest and helpful in assessing strengths and weaknesses.

After you have your own list and the lists of others, compare them and see if you see yourself as others see you. This is a simple exercise. It's not rocket science. It doesn't take a psychiatrist to obtain and evaluate such information. As you consider your list of possible occupations, ask yourself if you are well-suited to each choice based upon your results.

Chapter 6

So, What Kind of Work Should I Seek?

The Four Basic Types of Work

Remember, there are basically four types of work. I can't think of any job that would not fit into at least one of these categories. The first thing to consider is which of the following fits you best:

- Work that deals with people
- Work that deals with things
- Work that deals with data
- Work that deals with ideas

Developing Your List of Criteria

In this section, we will ask a series of questions regarding personal preferences. They are questions that have either opposite answers or "yes/no" answers. Make a list of answers to these questions, and then use them as a set of criteria by which you can evaluate any potential job. It is important to be completely honest with yourself as you answer each question with respect to each job you consider. Remember, you are the one who will be doing that job day in and day out—not your parents, not your friends—only you.

Following are 34 questions to ask yourself about your work preferences:

1. Do you want to be a boss or do you prefer working under a good boss?
2. Do you consider yourself to be a natural leader or a good follower?
3. Do you like to lead groups of people?
4. Would you prefer a job that is indoors or outdoors?
5. Do you like a blue collar or a white collar setting?
6. Would you prefer a manufacturing environment or an office environment?
7. Do you prefer to work independently or with a group?
8. Would you prefer to work with people or products?
9. Do you like to help people solve their problems?
10. Do you like to work with your hands or with your mind?
11. Do you like to work with computers?
12. Do you like detail work with numbers, figures, statistics, money, etc?
13. Do you like to analyze financial data?
14. Do you like to do the same basic work everyday or work with new projects?
15. Does it matter to you whether or not you work in an upscale office environment?
16. Do you like to be out and around town or work in the same place everyday?
17. Does out-of-town travel interest you, or do you want to work in the town where you live?
18. Would you prefer to go out and call on people or have them come to you?
19. Do you like to teach in your work, or do you find that monotonous or counter-productive?

20. Do you like competitive, even confrontational situations, or do you prefer a nonconfrontational environment?
21. Do you like paper-pushing work or hands-on work?
22. Do you like to work in an environment where you are surrounded by many people, or do you prefer a more solitary environment?
23. Do you like to meet with people on a one-to-one basis?
24. Do you like to talk on the phone?
25. Do you enjoy attending and participating in meetings?
26. Do you enjoy work that involves study and research?
27. Do you like to write reports, letters, and other business correspondence?
28. Do you like to write creatively in your work?
29. Do you like to speak to groups of people or meet with people individually?
30. Do you like to sell?
31. Do you like to be involved in and resolve conflicts?
32. Do you like to maintain or fix things?
33. Are you more comfortable working under clear direction, or do you prefer to set your own agenda and direct your own work?
34. Are you more comfortable making a known, fixed salary, or would you rather be paid based on incentives?

These are basic questions you need to consider in evaluating any career or job you consider. Once again, make sure you base your answers on your true opinions and preferences.

Make a list of the answers to each of these questions. This will be a good list of criteria for evaluating any job. In fact, you should give this a try. Take your list of criteria and evaluate your parents' jobs against this list and see how you come out. Then, evaluate some of the jobs on the following list against your set of criteria and see how this works. You may or may not truly know much about what people in these professions do. Just base your evaluation on what you do know and see what happens.

- Newspaper Reporter
- Computer Programmer
- Chemist
- Lawyer
- Chemical Plant Manager
- Department Store Manager
- Restaurant Manager
- Physician
- Teacher
- Stockbroker
- Insurance Sales
- Real Estate Broker
- Minister
- Entertainer
- Building Contractor
- Psychologist
- Investment Analyst
- Banker
- Editor

After you've evaluated a few of these jobs against the list, take your own list of possibilities and evaluate the answers against your answers to the questions.

Selecting Potential Job Titles

If you have decided on a general field you would like to work in or even a specific company you might like to work for, you need to zero in on specific jobs you might like to do. It really doesn't make much sense to go to a company and apply for a job without a specific job in mind. This is a big problem for people who major in very general fields.

Suppose, for example, you majored in business administration or management. You could probably handle or learn any office management job that any big company might have to offer, whether it be in banking, insurance, real estate, manufacturing, etc. If you would like to work for IBM or Ford or any other specific company, you must still tell them what you want to do. If you walk in and apply for a job, and they ask what job do you want to apply for, a nonspecific answer will not suffice. If you say, "Oh I'd just like to apply for any job that would be suitable for a person with a B.S. in Business, they'll simply file your application away in the local landfill.

Finding a specific Industry

If you have a degree in business or accounting or engineering, you still need to look at possible industries that utilize that educational background. A website like www.onetcenter.org/tools.html will have information that connects specific occupations with specific industries. That particular site is not easy to navigate, but it does have a great deal of information.

Another option is what I call "a trip through the yellow pages." Find a phone directory in a community where you would like to live. Look at the general index of businesses. There will be hundreds or thousands of categories, depending upon the size of the city. Each category on that huge list represents an industry or type of business where people work and earn their livelihoods. Take some time to look through the general index. Then take a lesson from the phone company and "let your fingers do the walking" through the yellow pages. You'll be amazed at the hundreds of industry options you would never have thought about. Each listing under each category represents a specific employer that hires people just like you!

Other sources for finding industries, businesses or professions of interest are the company directories at the public library. Directories like Dun & Bradstreet, Standard and Poors, and Thomas Register list every possible business or industry. The librarian will also help you with many other directories that are even more specific. As an example, every state will publish a manufacturer's directory for their state. They will also have directories for banks and financial institutions, insurance concerns, real estate organizations, etc. Most of these directories will have websites that will help, also.

As an example, go to the website for Thomas Register, www.thomasregister.com. Thomas Register is primarily a listing for manufacturers. There, you can select any product or service in the industrial or manufacturing realm. You can also locate organizations by company name or even brand names.

SIC Codes

In these directories, businesses will be listed by Standard Industrial Classification Codes or SIC Codes. Go to any search engine and type in the words, "sic codes," and you will find websites that list and explain the codes. Or, simply go to www.siccode.com. Look through the vast list of codes and you'll find another inexhaustible list of businesses. And remember, each of these types of businesses employ thousands and thousands of people.

Finding a Job Title

In order to find that specific job of interest, let me suggest
you start with the Sunday newspaper. Look in the
employment section and find out what jobs are advertised.
Your purpose, at this point, is not to apply for one of those
jobs, though there would be nothing wrong with doing so.
Your real purpose is to look at and evaluate the job titles and
the brief job descriptions. The reason the paper is such a
good place to look is that job descriptions are brief and
concise. That's because companies must pay by the column
inch to have that information in the paper, unlike the
Internet where they can describe a position in endless detail.

The next step would be to go to a major job board like
Monster or Yahoo or a local job board, type in the search
criteria that apply to you, and see what jobs pop up. For
example, you might type in the general title, "market
research" or "loan officer" or any other job and then see
what specific jobs appear. You may land on such titles as
"Program Manager," "Market Researcher," "Market Analyst,"
or "Account Manager." Look at the job descriptions and
evaluate them according to the list of criteria you developed
earlier in this chapter. Make a list of these specific titles of
interest.

The third step would be to go to a company website and
click on the link for career opportunities. Most big
companies have such links. For example, go to www.ibm.com.
On the home page, you will see a link that says, "Jobs at
IBM." Select the region and country and follow the links to
the "Find a Job" link. There you will see listings of many jobs

with appropriate job descriptions. Again, compare these jobs to the list of criteria you have selected. When you find job titles of interest, add these to your list.

Repeat this process with many companies. You will soon have a very full list of job title possibilities. A word of warning! Don't worry if the job requirements call for several years of experience you do not have. When you begin to inquire about specific jobs, you can refine your preference to jobs that lead up to the desired position. For example, if the job is for a Program Manager and requires many years of experience, you can look for Assistant Program Manager positions or inquire further as to which jobs can be found in the particular job track leading up to that position.

Finding Specific Entry Level Job Titles

After you have located these job titles, how do you go about finding the titles for entry-level jobs? Let's take the example from the previous paragraph. Suppose you have an accounting degree and you see a job ad for an Investment Analyst. Suppose that job looks like what you want to be doing, but requires five years experience. What you want to know is the jobs that lead up to Investment Analyst. What you need to do is pick up the phone and call someone in that position, if that is possible. I realize it is often very difficult to get inside a big organization where you don't know anyone. You might even contact a person in the Human Resources Department and see if they can help you with such information. Again, in this day when so many companies want you to talk to machines first, that can be a hurdle.

In the chapter on Networking, we'll talk about ways to get past those "screening barriers" and get to the people with whom you need to talk to get the information you need.

Part II

Networking:

The Most Effective Job Search Method

Chapter 7

Will Anybody Help Me Find a Job?

You are out of college, or soon will be. You've got an idea what you want to do. Now, you've just got to find a place to land. How are you going to do that? Well, you've got several options:

- You can go to the Internet
- You can answer ads in newspapers and journals
- You can go to recruiters
- You can start a personal marketing campaign
- You can network

All of these are good strategies. All of them have the possibility of working for you. All of them work for someone. But, as a new graduate, or soon-to-be new grad, I want to recommend one strategy in particular: **networking**. Surely you've heard of networking? It's a common buzzword in business circles. But, what exactly is it? In this chapter, I'll try to explain it to you as briefly as possible. I'll try to do this in such a way that you can start doing it today!

Have you ever been sitting around with friends talking about the process of finding a job when the name of some lucky, "already-employed" friend comes up—someone who seemed to find a job so easily? In discussing that person's situation, someone pops up and says, "Oh, he just got that job because he knew someone." If that's true, you just found a good example of what networking is all about. Usually, the person who made the statement is insinuating the fortunate friend just had a lucky break. And, the rest of you could never have that kind of luck, because you don't have the contacts that could land you a job.

Networking is getting a job because you know somebody. For you see, everybody knows somebody. In fact, almost everyone knows several "somebody's" who can help him. And, isn't that a great way to find a job? Actually, in most cases, it's the very best way to find a job.

What is a Network?

A network, simply stated is this—who you know and who they know! Networking is one friend helping another by introducing him to new friends who, in turn, can help you. Networking is asking people you know to help in your job search without directly asking them for a job. It's asking for advice and counsel, then asking them to point you toward others who, can likewise, give advice and counsel. Then, at some point, one of those people will have a job to offer you.

Networking is nothing new. As long as people have been forming associations, both informally and formally, they have been helping each other. If you are a member of a family, a club, a church, a class, a team, a company or any other kind of group of people with which you have something in common, you have people with whom you can network.

Think about your own personal network. You have your immediate family—your mom, dad, brothers and sisters. Then you have your aunts, uncles, and cousins. If you're in a fraternity or sorority, networking is one of the major purposes of the organization. That's why they call them "brothers" and "sisters." You also have classmates and other friends on that level. Consider professors you know well. Make a list of everyone on that first level of contacts.

Don't forget about professional associations. When I was majoring in chemistry in college, I was a member of the Student Chapter of the American Chemical Society. That affiliation allowed us to go to meetings of the regular ACS chapters.

In my current work, since I do recruiting for the paint and coatings industry, I have contacts in the Paint Society. Students are not only welcome at their meetings—they are **more than welcome!** The "old timers" in the society are flattered and honored when students and new graduates show an interest in their profession. It's an environment that is super-ripe for networking opportunities. If you participate in the society and ask a member for the opportunity to do some networking, they'll help you instantly. It will be the easiest networking contact you'll ever make. The moral to the story is simply: find and join a professional association in the field of your college major. Go to the meetings. Be active. You'll find yourself in the company of networking giants who will help you along the way.

Six Degrees of Separation

One of the interesting concepts that has been popular for the past few years is "six degrees of separation." This means you can be connected to anyone in the world through six different people. For example, you may not know the President of the United States. But you probably know someone who knows your congressman. Even if your congressman does not know the President well (he's probably met him officially, but may not truly know him), he knows a leader of the House of Representatives that does know the President. They are three degrees or three levels removed.

In the case of networking, you are seeking business relationships with people who are only one or two levels removed. For example, your father is one level removed. Your father's insurance agent is two levels removed. Your job is to establish a "friend" relationship with that insurance agent. At the point he becomes your friend, he is no longer two levels removed. He is a first level relationship, who may be able to point you to other people who can help you.

Networking is a two-way street. Just as you need people to help you, there are others whom you can help. You can refer them to people you know. One day when you are established in your career, others will be coming to you for networking help. You'll want to be there for them, as well.

How Does the Process Work?

Networking is something you should start doing right now, wherever you are in your journey of life. It is something that should never stop. And remember, networking applies to all aspects of your life, not just the task of finding a job. It is useful in your social life, your political life, your avocational life, and your family life.

For now, let's talk about how networking can be used in a job search. There are two primary job markets out there:

- The public job market
- The hidden job market

The public job market consists of jobs that are posted or advertised, whether internally or externally. They are listed in classified ads, company Internet sites, and public Internet job boards such as Monster, Yahoo, etc. They are also given out to recruiters.

The hidden job market consists of those jobs that are there, but not yet posted or never to be posted. It is a huge hassle for a company to advertise a job, receive and evaluate applications, and wade slowly through the interview process. It's also a huge expense. If an organization can find people without going through all that, they love to do so. So, if the boss doesn't want to go to the public marketplace, keeping the job in the hidden marketplace is a good idea. Or, perhaps the position is approved, but he doesn't have to fill it right away. He simply wants to wait until a good candidate appears and then work with that person. Another scenario may be that a position is being conceived and developed in the mind of the boss. It may be a job that will be posted in the future, unless a good candidate falls right into the boss's lap.

Let me illustrate this with a story from my family. My oldest son is an example of how networking and the hidden marketplace can work. When he was 16, he wanted to find a summer job. At that time, we were members of a small church with less than 100 people. He mentioned his intention to several people in the church. A couple of them worked for a small firm that did telephone customer support for Hewlett-Packard. They knew Andy, so they suggested he come in and talk to them. Since they knew quite a lot about him and what kind of person he was, there was no need to go through the usual routine of screening. They hired him immediately, and he went to work.

Some time later, that group lost its contract with H-P. Meanwhile, two of the people in that organization had gone to work for a larger company that had a high tech customer support department. They were looking for some good people. But, this job was on the hidden job market. They were looking for a warm contact, someone they knew about. Andy simply called them to ask if they knew of anything that would be right for him. They told him about their position. He asked when he should come for the interview. They said, "You don't need to come for an interview. We already know you."

They knew of his abilities and his track record of performance. What else could they learn from an interview? They were not evaluating a stranger. They were hiring a friend. Eventually, that company was sold to a larger company and most of the staff was laid off. However, that job led to an internship with Bank of America, which turned into his first job out of college. He has been there ever since.

How did all of this get started? It started with networking, though neither he nor I actually knew what networking was all about at the time. One interesting point is that we were in a tiny, little church, not a great big mega-church with thousands of people. The opportunity started with just a few people he already knew. And it can work that way for you, too. You don't have to know a lot of people. The people you know don't even have to be big shots. They don't have to be in big organizations. Companies always prefer to hire friends rather than strangers. And, a friend of a good employee is more likely to slip into the role of "friend of the company" than a total stranger who applies from the outside.

What Is the Purpose of Job Search Networking?

Why is networking such an effective tool for the job search process? It is effective because it allows you to make contact with people who can offer you a job in an indirect, yet personal, nonthreatening manner. It is nonthreatening because you are not going to ask these people for a job. You are simply going to seek advice and direction.

But you may say, "I'm not the outgoing type of person who can approach people very easily. It won't work for me." You don't have to be outgoing to talk to people you know. In this type of networking, you're not approaching strangers. You're talking to friends, and friends of friends!

For college students and new graduates, networking is particularly easy. In fact, it's easier for this group than for any other group of people. You see, people in business like to help young people who are trying to get started in life. When you go to them, you honor them by asking them for advice and direction. You're giving them an opportunity to be a good Boy Scout or Girl Scout. You're allowing them an opportunity to do their "good deed for the day." When you go to older, more mature people, they enjoy giving you "fatherly" or "motherly" advice. It takes them back to the time when they were in your shoes trying to get started. Believe me, 95 percent of them will do everything they possibly can to help you! So what are you waiting for? It's time to get started!

Why People Will Meet With You

Remember, people will meet with you for several reasons:

- They like to help other people
- They like to say "yes" when it comes to helping others
- They like to be recognized for their experience and expertise
- They have been in your shoes before
- They will be in your shoes needing the help of others in the future

When you network, you must not expect immediate gratification. Meeting with people takes time. Establishing relationships takes time. You may be able to find any old job more quickly through other job search strategies. But, networking will usually find you the best possible job through people you know, who will view you as a friend.

Chapter 8

How Do I Define My Network?

Networking starts when you sit down and determine who is in your network. Remember, it starts with the people closest to you—people you already know.

Here are some places you can identify your network contacts:

- Your immediate family
- Your extended family
- Friends of your family
- Fraternity or Sorority
- Company alumni (former employees of a company)
- Your professors and instructors
- Professional associations
- Church family
- Co-workers at present or past jobs
- Clubs you belong to (present and past)
- Neighbors
- Sports teams
- Political connections
- Parents from your children's school
- Professionals you deal with (doctors, dentists, lawyers, accountants, insurance)

You should evaluate all these sources and make a list of names of people you know well enough to call. If you have a contacts database such as ACT or even a program like OUTLOOK, establish a record for each contact and make notes when you call them. Even a simple card file system will work just fine.

I am writing this from the point of view of a person who has been in the professional and executive recruiting field. My business is one big networking system. On my database, I make a record of every contact. Each person I call goes on my database, and I make notes on the computer of every phone call. When I call a person on the database, I note the date of the call, the reason for the call and the results of the call. Whether you use a computerized system or an index card system, you should do the same with each person on your networking database. I also have a simple cataloging system, so I can easily bring up any contact or group of contacts by searching the file based on a four-digit code. You could set up your own coding system to help you categorize your contacts.

Chapter 9

Be Prepared: The Thirty-Second Speech and the Two-Minute Speech

As you meet people with whom you can network, you should always be prepared to tell them something about yourself in a clear, concise manner. You should be prepared to ask them to help you. You should be prepared to give them a reason to help you. Two of the tools you need to carry with you at all times are your "thirty-second presentation" and your "two-minute presentation."

The Thirty-Second Presentation

When you meet a person and they say, "Tell me something about yourself," what do you do? What do you say? If you're not prepared, you probably start off with something like, "Well, er, um, uh…" and it goes downhill from there. Don't let that happen to you. BE PREPARED! If you're a new or recent graduate or a soon-to-be graduate, your thirty second presentation should tell an inquirer these basic points:

- Your name
- Your educational preparation
- Your job function or intended job function
- The industry
- Your geographic preference
- Your target company or company type

Here's an example of a script I might have used when I was looking for my first career job:

> My name is Fred Cooper. I'm a recent graduate of Trinity University in San Antonio with a masters degree in health care administration. I've also served a one-year internship at Memorial Baptist Hospital System in Houston. I'm looking for an entry-position in hospital administration anywhere in the State of Texas.

If you have some job experience under your belt, the presentation would be slightly different. It should include:

- Your name
- Your label (your occupation or title)
- Your job function
- The industry
- Your geographic preference
- Target companies or types of companies

So, if I were giving my thirty-second presentation after my first five years of experience, I might have said something like this:

> My name is Fred Cooper. I've been an assistant administrator of All Saints Hospital in Fort Worth, Texas for the past five years with experience in both the professional and administrative areas of the hospital. I'm looking for a vice president position with a major hospital or a position as CEO of a small hospital anywhere in the State of Texas.

You'd be surprised how few people are actually prepared to give such a simple presentation when they have the opportunity. If you are prepared, and can make this presentation well, you will be perceived as a person with excellent communication skills. The person who sought this information will know that you have good grasp of where you want to go and what you want to be!

So, write this presentation now! Learn it. Say it over and over until you could say it in your sleep! Practice it on your family and friends. Be prepared to use it whenever the opportunity arises. And, if you're prepared, you'll be astonished at how often the opportunity will arise.

The Two-Minute Presentation

In presenting yourself in other situations, you should have a two-minute presentation. In this little speech, you must include these points:

1. Your education
2. Your related work experience, if any
3. Your current status and career ambition
4. A question asking his opinion

If you are not seeking your very first position, then you will include information about any other related career experience you have. You need not include noncareer experience, such as college jobs either sacking groceries, waiting tables or digging ditches.

Here's an example of a one-to-two-minute presentation:

> I'm a new college graduate with a degree in business administration from the University of Texas. In college, I was particularly interested in marketing courses as well as courses in business communications. During my college years, I held part time jobs in two real estate companies, where I learned the basic workings of the real estate business, including property listing

and agency activities. I also worked for an experienced commercial appraisal consultant and learned how to prepare various types of real estate appraisal reports, including all of the statistical and demographic data that must go into such presentations. At the present time, I am looking for my first career position. I am interested in an office management position where I can best utilize the organizational and communication skills I learned through my education and previous job experiences. At this point in time, I am open to many options and am wondering if you could help me in refining my search and developing some good options for me?

Your presentation will vary depending upon the person to whom it is being directed. This is a presentation you should learn, as an actor would learn a long passage in a play. You should rehearse with your buddy and several friends or family members so it will go smoothly, when you present it in a real networking situation.

Partners in the Job Search Process

Another part of the preparation process is practicing every aspect of your job search activities and reviewing your strategy for every step. You should seek good counsel and support in everything you do.

When you develop your 30-second speech and your two-minute speech, you need to practice them. You need to rehearse! When you go to a movie and see an effectively produced scene, you can be sure they simply didn't pass out the scripts and shoot the scene! You can be sure the actors studied and learned their lines before showing up for rehearsal. You can be sure the director had exhaustive rehearsals before calling in the production crew.

In the '80s, the most popular TV series was a show called "**Dallas.**" Much of the show was actually filmed in Dallas, and, if you were at the right place at the right time, you could watch them shoot the scenes. One day, I was shopping at a major downtown department store. As I was walking out, I noticed a film crew in the cosmetics department. Lo and behold, they were filming a scene for one of the episodes. It was a short scene that probably took less than 30 seconds of TV time. But, they did it over, and over, and over again! Even after they had rehearsed the scene, they still practiced and repeated it with the cameras rolling.

If you are serious about your job search, should you be any less diligent about your preparation? You need to practice your speeches with your friends, so you can deliver them effectively when the opportunity arises.

The Buddy System

As you begin to identify people in your network, I am going to suggest you start with one essential and important person—your buddy. When I was a kid, I went to a summer camp where we swam in a small lake. To keep us safe, the lifeguard used "the buddy system." Each camper was paired up with another person. We were to swim together and be together at all times. When the lifeguard blew his whistle, each pair of buddies had to stop what they were doing, join hands and hold their hands up in the air. Each person in the pair had to account for the other and be responsible for his welfare!

The most important person in your network should be your buddy. You should work together in the job search process. You should support each other, encourage each other, motivate each other, and keep each other going when the times gets tough. This is the person with whom you will practice your marketing scripts and presentations, your telephone calls, and the "dry runs" of your meetings. This is the one who will critique your resume and your marketing letters. Your buddy may be a friend who is also in the job search process. It could be a brother or sister. It could be an older friend who has already walked this path before you. It could be your mentor, if you have one.

Networking Groups

Another place to find a buddy is at a networking group. You will find networking groups at various places. In some newspapers, they are listed as job clubs. Many large churches have networking groups. Ask the career counselor at your college if they have or know of networking groups. If you can find one, you will surely locate one or more buddies to encourage you and help you in your networking and job search activities. There are even some networking groups to be found on the Internet, though it is always best to have a real, live person to whom you can be accountable.

Chapter 10

How Do I Get the Networking Process Started?

There are several objectives in setting up networking contacts:

- You want to establish target companies in your field of interest
- You want to find people who work in your target field
- You want to ask these people all about what they do
- You want to ask if they think you would fit in the field
- You want to ask them to refer you to other people and companies they know in the field
- You want to offer to do something for them

How to Set Up a Networking Meeting

People You Know

It starts with people you already know. These people can introduce you to other people whom you want to meet— people who are active in your field of interest.

You start by matching your list of contacts with your list of companies and industries. With the sources of contacts we have discussed, it is likely you would have access to someone who would know an appropriate contact in almost any field. There may not be any direct matches. But, there will surely be some indirect matches. Also, several of your friends will have contacts in areas you may never have considered.

For example, you may be interested in finding people in the field of petroleum accounting. Maybe none of your friends knows anyone in that direct field; however, they may know someone who is an engineer or a geologist for an oil company. That person will know someone in the accounting area. Or, perhaps none of your friends knows anyone in the petroleum industry. They may, however, know someone in accounting in another field like nonprofit foundations or paper manufacturing or any other industry. Maybe you should be exploring ideas like that, also.

It is not hard to ask people you know well for this kind of information. Call everyone on your list and ask who they know in the area you are choosing to explore. Make a list of those contacts. Prioritize the list. Now that you've spoken with that first level of contacts, you're ready to begin speaking to level number two.

Your Telephone Presentation

Write down your presentation and practice it before you call. You should practice your telephone presentation with family members or roommates or close friends. You say, "That sounds funny, making a telephone call from a script." It's not funny at all. I've been in the recruiting business for 25 years, and I still write scripts for presenting candidates and recruiting candidates for companies. There are also times when I "wing it" without a script. I can tell you from my experience I always make a better telephone presentation when I use a script. The problem is NOT the use of a script. A problem only occurs when it SOUNDS LIKE you're using a script.

I recently received a political telephone solicitation. It sounded like a third grader was reading the script. The call was probably being made by a minimum wage telephone clerk who had no interest whatsoever in the outcome of the call. She was just doing a job to collect a check. If you will practice your presentation as though you were giving an important speech, you can make a very effective call and say every single word that needs to be said. If you don't use a script, you'll end up leaving out important information, perhaps even the most important points. You'll end up kicking yourself because you blew an opportunity to make a truly effective call!

What Do I Say in the Request for a Meeting?

There are several points you need to make in your **request for a meeting**:

- You need to introduce yourself and tell them who referred you to them
- You need to tell them you are trying to get started in life and that you are looking at different career opportunities
- You need to tell them, "I am not asking for a job, but I do want to network with you" (In this day and time, people will know what you mean by that)
- You need to explain the purpose of the meeting
- You need to ask for an appointment
- You need to thank them

Now, let's look at a one of those points—the purpose of the meeting, in a little more detail. You need to tell them it is your purpose to talk to people in their field of work. You will want to:

- Ask them what they do in their work
- Tell them a little about yourself and see if they think you would fit
- Ask for their advice and counsel in seeking work

By preparing them for what you want to discuss and asking only for 15 to 20 minutes of their time, they will be much more favorable to granting you an appointment.

Here's a sample script:

> "Hello, Mr. Smith. My name is Fred Cooper. I was referred to you by Joe Jones, my marketing professor at the University of Texas. I'm in the process of trying to get started in my career. I'm calling to see if I could set up a brief 20-minute meeting with you. I'm not asking for a job, but I do want to network with you. In our meeting, I'd like to ask you a few questions about your work, and how you got started. I'd like to tell you a little bit about myself, and ask some advice and counsel in the kind of work you think would be best for me. Would it be possible for me to meet with you next week?"

That's what you should say. Those are the essential elements of the request for a networking meeting. Your exact script doesn't have to read exactly that way, but those major points should be included. And, once again, let me emphasize the importance of writing it down and practicing it.

Perhaps everyone will not grant you an appointment. Don't be discouraged. Keep calling down that list. You will experience success in getting appointments. In fact, most people will agree to meet with you.

What If They Can't Meet In Person?

There are some good reasons why everyone will not be able to meet with you in person:

- Their schedule is truly full, and they don't have time for a face to face meeting
- Their company setup is not amenable for receiving visitors from the outside (such as a highly secure company environment)
- The contact is in another city, and a personal meeting is not possible

The telephone is still a good way to conduct a networking meeting. If the face to face meeting is not possible, ask if you can have a few minutes of their time on the phone. Ask them when the best time would be. It is best to schedule a specific time to talk when they are free. They may tell you that RIGHT NOW is as good a time as any. Or, you may ask them if they could take a few minutes RIGHT NOW. Of course, it is important that you be prepared for the instant meeting, if it should work out that way.

Chapter 11

The Networking Meeting: What Do I Do When I Get There?

Objectives of the Networking Meeting

There are several things you want to accomplish in a networking meeting. You should:

- Introduce yourself well
- Obtain information about the interviewer's job and company
- Seek advice concerning your situation
- Seek referrals in target companies
- Add to your list of target companies or potential employers
- Uncover a hidden job there or at another company.
- Practice the interviewing process
- Share information with the person with whom you are meeting

What To Do at a Networking Meeting

A networking meeting is, in some ways, like a job interview, but in most ways, it is very different. For one thing, it's an informal situation in the mind of the person with whom you are meeting. (You have already told him you're not there to ask for a job). It's important to be there on time, which means five minutes early. You should definitely dress properly, as if you were dressing for an interview.

At this point, let me say something about what to wear. In years past, this was a "no-brainer." A man would wear a suit. A woman would wear a suit. PERIOD. That was it. Today, it's a bit different. If you can find out how people dress in that organization without too much fuss, then do so. Generally, businesses go with business casual which means wool type slacks and a nice long sleeve shirt for men and an appropriate dress for women. If you are a young person just finishing college, business casual is fine for most situations. If you want to play it safe without being too formal, wear gray slacks, a navy blue blazer, a white shirt, and a red tie. You can always shed the jacket, if the situation warrants.

What To Do When You Get There

When you arrive at the appointment, remember to treat every person respectfully. Even the lowest person on the company's totem pole, who has a reason not to like you, could prevent you from getting a job there, if you should be so fortunate as to uncover a hidden job.

When you go into the appointment, you should let the interviewer know you appreciate his giving you the time and establish your agenda for the meeting. Here are the general points of the agenda:

- Break the ice! (introductions, establish rapport)
- Set the agenda
- Give your introductory presentation
- Ask for opinions and advice
- Present your list of target companies and get additional referrals
- Ask what you can do for him or her
- Present your resume at the end

Let's consider these points in more detail.

Breaking the Ice

This is, arguably, the most important part of any meeting of any kind. Much has been written about the significance of the first 10 seconds of any meeting. That's when you make eye contact, shake hands, and utter those first words. That's something that really cannot be scripted. Yes, I could tell you to give a firm, but not bone-crushing handshake (no limp dishrag handshake). I could tell you to smile. I could tell you be pleasant. But, the most important thing I can tell you is to simply be yourself. There's something that happens between two individuals during that critical period of time that really cannot be predicted. I call it an exchange of spirits. Without wanting to be too mystical about that, let me just say that when you first meet someone, you just know whether you like them or not! It has to do with the feel of the handshake, the look in your eye, and the sound of your voice that is as characteristic as the way you look. Everyone has certain preferences. Some people have the innate ability to "meet people well."

My mother-in-law was a pleasant, but not too outgoing person. It was hard for people to make a good first impression on her. One day, a stockbroker friend came to our home. We simply introduced him to her. He greeted her in his usual way, and we went about our business. After he left, my mother-in-law remarked, "I like that young man." It was a highly unusual response. I had never heard her say that about anyone before. As I analyzed it, there was something about his "10-second icebreaker" that just set him apart from everyone else. It had to do with his countenance, his natural sincerity, tone of voice and manners.

Summing up the icebreaker, let me say, it's not something that can be contrived or acted out. Furthermore, you never know the kind of person the interviewer is, or the kind of person he likes. So, just be yourself and do the best you can!

The other part of the icebreaker is the establishing of rapport. You might say something nice about the mutual friend who introduced you. If you know the person went to a certain college, or that he loves golfing, hunting, fishing, or anything else, this makes a good bridge-building topic.

Set the Agenda

After the icebreaker, thank the interviewer for his time and set the agenda.

These are the three main points of your agenda:

1. Present your background and desires
2. Learn about what he does
3. Lay out your strategy and seek his advice

Here's an example of what you might say in presenting your agenda:

> "I appreciate your granting me this time, as I know you are a very busy person. What I want to do today is to tell you something about my background and my career desires. I'd like to learn something about what you do, how you made the decision to choose this line of work and see what you think of my plan for seeking a position."

Ask for Opinions and Advice

This is the main part of your meeting. You want to ask several questions about his or her career. Here are some good questions:

- How did you choose this business?
- What is the career path to your current position?
- What entry-level position should you seek to get started?
- What is an average workday?
- Will this be a good career for the future?
- What do you like most about your work?
- What do you like least about your work?
- Would you choose this line of work if you were in my shoes starting today?
- From what you know about me, do you think this would be a good career for me?

Make a list of these questions and **take the list with you** to the informational interview. It will be hard to remember everything you might want to ask if you don't write the questions down. Also, it will show you do your homework, and you respect his time.

Present Your List of Target Companies and Get Referrals

In this phase of the meeting, you should present the target industries and target companies you have identified. Have these written down as well. Ask him if he knows of additional companies or organizations that should be on the list. Ask him if he could recommend similar industries where your abilities might fit. Also, ask if he knows anyone at any of these companies.

In searching for contacts, don't forget to ask where he worked in his previous position, and ask for contacts in that organization.

It is very important to ask for his permission to use his name in contacting people. If you feel comfortable in doing so, ask if he would be willing to call some of these people and introduce you prior to your making contact. (This will make all the difference in the world in the way you are received). You won't always be able to get this kind of help, but if you can, don't bypass the opportunity. Additionally, you should ask him if he has any advice for your job search.

Ask What You Can Do For Them

Networking should always be a two-way street. You should seek to help the interviewer any way you can. Perhaps you feel you have little to offer at this stage. This is not necessarily the case. In the course of your job search, you may have picked up some interesting and even valuable news or information about the industry. This might include information about mergers, government actions that would affect the industry, information about competition, or information about important people in the industry. This will be gratefully received and appreciated.

Also, you should ask if there is anything you can do to help him in some way. Remember, networking works both ways and, if the potential employer feels you are trying to help him, he will be more inclined to help you!

Present Your Resume

You should certainly have a copy of your resume with you. The time to present it is at the end of the meeting, not the beginning. There are some basic reasons for this:

- Presenting it at the beginning would give the impression you are asking for a job (you indicated when you made the appointment you are not asking for a job)
- Presenting the resume initially will focus the interviewer's attention on your resume rather than your agenda—anything you present might set a different agenda for your meeting
- If he does have a hidden job opportunity, he will be more interested in considering you after you have met with him for informational purposes, and the presentation of the resume will be more timely

Follow-Up to the Meeting

When a person grants you a networking meeting, he has done a really big favor for you. That should not go unrecognized. You should send a **handwritten** thank you note **as soon as the interview is over. You write it that day, not the next day.** You say, why not an e-mail message instead? It's much faster and easier. There is nothing wrong with that approach, but a handwritten note gets more attention. It takes much more time and effort. People receive many e-mails in a day. They receive very few handwritten thank you notes, and they remember the ones they do get. Such a note will set up you apart from the crowd, the ones who take the easiest road.

Additionally, you should call your contact back in a week or so to thank him. You should especially do so after you follow-up any leads he has given you. He will WANT TO KNOW the results of the time he spent with you and the advice he gave you. This will NOT be an imposition to him. In reemphasizing the importance of this, let me say your natural inclination and thought will be not to bother the person anymore, after he gave his time so graciously. NOT TRUE! He will be glad you followed-up, and when you do, he may even have some additional help for you! In fact, he will be even more likely to help you after the follow-up because he will know you better and will see you have taken his advice seriously.

Let me illustrate this with some personal observations. As a professional recruiter, my first obligation is to the company that hires me to find an employee. My obligation is NOT to the job seeker. Hopefully, I can help people seeking jobs, but my obligation is to the one who pays me. Therefore, there are many people whom I cannot help in any way other than to give advice on finding a job through other strategies. I do this very frequently. On many occasions, my friends refer people to me for help and advice—people whom I could never place in a job. I then participate in a networking interview with their friend. Actually, I enjoy doing this, as do most people. But, when I do give my valuable time, I want to know the results of my advice. I want to hear back from the person. I want to know if he took my advice. I want to know if they tried to do what I advised them to do!

And, how many people do you think ever call me back? The answer is that almost NO ONE ever calls me back. Maybe they think they're troubling me and don't want to take any more time. The opposite is true. I DO want to talk to them again. When they don't, I feel they probably did not appreciate what I had to say.

At the risk of sounding like a broken record, let me emphasize once again, if you don't follow-up on your networking meetings, you're shooting yourself in the foot. Contrary to what you might think, that person has given his time and has taken an interest in you. He wants to know how you're coming along. Not responding robs him of personal satisfaction, and it deprives you of further cementing a networking relationship that can be profitable for years to come. Remember, one good contact with a person is a good thing, but it will quickly be forgotten. Two contacts further seal the relationship. After three good contacts, you have forged a friendship that will not be forgotten. So, stay in touch with people who help you!

Networking on the Telephone

You will not always be able to set face to face appointments for networking; however, you can network over the phone. You can ask for a telephone appointment and raise the same questions you would ask in person. If you are working through a mutual friend, this method can be almost as effective. If you are a person who does especially well on the telephone, the results of the call can be excellent. It is important, however, to make a follow-up phone call, since making a lasting relationship over the phone is more difficult and requires more than one visit.

Chapter 12

Networking with Strangers: How Can I Be Effective With People I Don't Know?

Networking is always easiest and best when you are talking with people you know or people they know. But, if you have the guts and the gall to do so, you can establish contacts with people you don't know! (I recognize the fact that most people would feel uncomfortable doing this and that they prefer the safety of approaching people through more standard means). If, however, you are willing to be a little bit bold and brash, the opportunities that can open up to you are virtually limitless!

One of the things you were seeking from your warm and friendly list of networking contacts was their paths of progression to their present positions. You asked them to tell you how to get started, what jobs to seek first, and what jobs to move into.

In the chapter on selecting a target job title, we talked about contacting people in companies to find out what they do. Also, we sought the entry-level titles leading to their job. Remember, I said we would discuss this further in the chapter on Networking. Well, here we are!

Networking with Strangers

In order to network with someone you don't know, you have to know his or her title. You have to know what he does. Then, you need to call the target company and:

- Find the name of the person with that title, or
- Just ask to speak with a person in that position.

Sometimes this can be extremely easy. If you are interested in the automobile business and want to speak with the sales manager of an agency, all you have to do is pick up the phone, dial the number, and ask for the sales manager. You will be connected with no hassle whatsoever. If you are interesting in retail marketing and want to talk to a department head at a department store, all you have to do is ask. You will be connected. Then, you can start your networking discussion.

But, what if you want to talk to an aerospace engineer at a high-tech, high-security defense contractor that works on top-secret projects? What if you want to talk to an actuary at a large insurance company? What if you want to talk to a director of software development for a large bank? What if you want to talk to an agent inside the IRS? Chances are, the only telephone number you can find is the one that goes to Customer Service. Another possibility is that the telephone receptionist does not have a list of titles and can only connect you to people whose names you know. That receptionist is trained to screen you out and to direct you only to places like Human Resources, Community Relations or Customer Service. You probably won't be able to get inside by walking through the "front door." You need to enter through the "back door," the "employees' entrance."

Getting into the "Back Door"

There are several ways to legitimately get around the barriers at the reception desk or the company telephone receptionist and talk to the people in the company with whom you need to network. Here are some of the options:

- Find news stories about companies and note the names given
- Find journal or magazine articles and note the names and companies of the authors
- Look up corporate alumni websites and find the names of former employees
- Check out your college alumni association
- Find association directories and note names of people who work in target companies
- Check out advertising flyers for conventions and trade shows and note the names of the speakers, who are being publicized for the meeting
- Call the company after hours, dial random extensions and get names from their voice mail messages, to be followed-up the next day.

Let me comment briefly on some of these approaches. Your best friend in seeking this information will be a good librarian at any college or public library. Go to the library and tell the librarian you are looking for stories about people who work at General Motors or Sears or Citibank. That person will be able to generate that information for you and/or tell you how to find it for yourself.

As for information in journals and trade shows, let me give you an example from my own experience. I have been placing people in the Paint and Coatings Industry for over twenty years. Every year, there are several conventions, trade shows, and educational meetings held on an annual or even semi-annual basis. One of those meetings is called "The High Solids Symposium" sponsored by the University of Southern Mississippi. Many years ago, I simply called the University and asked them to send me the promotional flyer for that meeting. They were delighted to do so. In fact, they placed me on their mailing list and send me the flyer every year. On that flyer, I find the names of several dozen people who are presenting educational papers at the meeting. Just about every major company in the industry is represented on that list. If I want to find a direct contact at Dow Chemical Company, I will find one or more names on that list. All I have to do is call the company and ask for that person by name. He or she will then direct me to other people.

On Corporate Alumni sites, you will find the names of former employees. Call them, tell them why you are calling and the type of job information you seek. Ask them for the names of people with whom you can network in their former company. In most cases, they will be an excellent source of names for you to call. They will understand and identify with your situation and your plight and will be happy to help you out.

When you are able to contact a person in that ultimate target position, tell him who you are and that you are seeking a career doing what he does. Ask about his path of progression and what entry level positions you should seek in his company. You may identify several possible job titles that lead where you want to go. You may be able, then, to specify several appropriate jobs.

What to say on a "Cold" Networking Call

When you contact someone you don't know, you must realize this is not a "warm contact." It is a "cold call." The first thing he will want to know is, "How did you get my name?" Tell him! Tell him the truth. Say, "I saw your name in the 'Such and Such Magazine" or "I saw your name on a speakers' list for the Widget Makers Convention," or "I saw your name in the newspaper." If you obtained his name through a cold telephone call, tell him that! You can say, "I simply called several random numbers in the company and asked around until I got your name." (In most cases, they'll be tickled and impressed with your ingenuity and spunk). If someone on an alumni list referred you to him, it is best not to use a referral name unless you have permission. Simply tell him truthfully how you obtained the name.

Will you ever be rejected using such an approach? On rare occasion, you will be! But, finding cold marketing contacts requires a "thick skin." If you are rejected, don't be discouraged. Simply move on to the next call.

In almost every case, when you tell your contact why you are calling, he will be receptive. Here's the outline of what to say:

- Give your thirty-second introductory speech
- Ask if you can speak to him for just a few minutes.
- Ask the same questions you would ask in a regular networking conversation. (In most cases, you will ask only two or three of those questions. Usually the question about entry-level positions will be the most important one).
- Ask if you could send your resume.
- Ask for referrals to other people in the company or other companies.
- If the call has gone well, ask if you could call again when you have additional questions.
- Ask for an e-mail address.
- In a few cases, where you feel it is appropriate, ask if you could schedule a face to face networking appointment.

Follow-Up for the Cold Networking Call

Whenever you have a successful marketing call, follow-up with a Thank You e-mail message. In this case, e-mail is usually better than the personal, handwritten note you would send after a regular networking appointment. If he gave you permission to call again, do it!

Cold Call Marketing is not easy. Most people simply cannot or will not do it. But, if you're one of those who can, you can achieve some amazing results. If you want to go into sales, you should certainly be able to make such calls. If you can't, then you should ask if you have what it takes to go into sales! We'll talk more about these types of contacts in the chapter on Personal Marketing.

Chapter 13

Maintaining Your Network: What Do I Do After My Networking Meetings?

Keeping Up With Your Network

What do you do with all the names in your personal network? Do you just discard them after you've talked with the people? Of course not! You need to keep track of these people. It can be as simple as a card file. Here is the information you should include:

- Name
- Title
- Contact information (address, phone, e-mail)
- Company
- Date of Initial Contact
- Referred by
- Notes regarding his job
- Notes regarding his advice
- Referrals (companies and individuals)
- Follow-up dates
- General notes

Perhaps the most important section is the "General Notes." Here, you should keep a running log or diary of every meeting or conversation. I do this on every call I make. (You'll be amazed how impressed a person will be when, at some time in the future, even years later, you can refer back to a specific comment that person made in a previous meeting or conversation).

Better yet, get some contact software. There's no reason why a person graduating from college and entering the workplace in this day and time should not automate this process. If you use Microsoft Outlook, which comes on most computers, that will work fine. If you want to be a little more sophisticated, you can use Access or Excel and develop your own format. These also come bundled with most computers. Another good program is ACT, a prepackaged contact management program. Microsoft has just come out with a program called One Note. There are many others, too.

By establishing your networking contacts on a good database, you can more easily access them and stay in touch. You can periodically send e-mails to individuals or entire groups to keep them informed as to your whereabouts and activities. You should go through your list of names periodically and determine if there is anything you can do to help anyone on that list. Remember, networking is a two-way street!

Perhaps you know a piece of industry information that could be valuable to one of your contacts. Perhaps, you know of a job or business opportunity that would be valuable to them. Maybe you can send some business their way. They will always be grateful. Also, it won't be too long before their company will be sold, downsized, or eliminated, and they will want to network with you. I know that sounds farfetched at the beginning of your career. But, time passes quickly, and it won't be long before you will be in a position to help your friends.

Other Uses for Networking

We have been talking about networking as it applies to the job search process, but that is only one application for networking. Networking is also valuable for finding customers or clients, for social contacts, for political help (whether that be business or governmental politics), or for help for a special need in your family or personal life.

One of my first networking card files was my wedding invitation file. My wife and I have been married for over 26 years, and I still use the list today. Your database should be cataloged or coded in such a way that you can always identify groups within your database. This can also be done by the use of keywords. For example, if you are identifying people by their work, the word "engineer" or, more specifically, "chemical engineer" might be the keyword or words you would use to identify the entire group on your networking database.

Your network will be a valuable resource for your entire life. The earlier you start developing and keeping track of your network, the more valuable it will be. Also, if you are keeping it on the computer, don't forget to back it up and periodically make a copy on a disk. Your network will be one of your most valuable possessions in years to come.

Part III

Other Methods for Finding a Job

Chapter 14

How Do I Find the Job I Want?

There are several methods you can use to find a job once you have decided the kind of job to seek. These include:

- Newspaper and Magazine ads
- Internet Sources
- Job Fairs
- Internships
- Temporary Employment
- Networking
- Personal Search Methods
- Search and Employment Agencies

Remember, we discussed the two job markets: public and private. The public job market includes advertised jobs, posted jobs and some agency jobs. Public jobs have always been available through what I call the "job clearinghouse." The job clearinghouse represents the marketplace where employers and job seekers can find each other. There has always been a clearinghouse. In the past, prior to the Internet, the clearinghouse included advertising sources, such as newspapers and magazines, as well as agency postings. Today, it also includes the various Internet options, including websites like Monster, Yahoo, Hotjobs, Dice, and thousands of job boards run by newspapers, trade associations, and others. It also includes jobs posted on websites by thousands of individual companies. Agency postings include things like private employment agencies, state employment commissions, and federal job postings, such as those found on the O*Net website. Some search agency jobs are public and some are hidden.

For example, a company may give a job order to several agencies in hopes that qualified candidates will be available through their listings. In other cases, the company may give a job order to agencies to keep the job out of the public marketplace. If the job were open to the public marketplace, the company would be bombarded with applications, which would make the job screening process too burdensome.

Let me give you an example of this. Some time ago, a building products manufacturing company came to me seeking a specific type of mechanical engineer. They looked on a couple of big Internet job boards and were inundated with hundreds of resumes from nonqualified engineers. Their small personnel department could not screen that many resumes effectively. (It would be easy to pass over the good resumes in a large stack). Therefore, they asked me to take up the search, knowing I would submit only carefully recruited candidates. I did not advertise. I contacted only people who were truly qualified. (That's what recruiters do). Therefore, the job was removed from the public market and made available on the hidden market only to people I approached.

The hidden job market is accessed by networking, personal job searches (a form of networking), and behind-the-scenes sources, such as vendors and friends of the company. As discussed in the chapter on networking, a large percentage of jobs are hidden. Companies choose not to make them public in hopes that qualified candidates will network their way in, or friends will recommend candidates. They also utilize search firms to source and present very carefully selected candidates.

Newspaper and Magazine Ads

Perhaps, this is the oldest method of job search. As long as printed media has existed, there has been employment advertising. Almost everyone, at one time or other, has had the experience of reading through the "help wanted" ads and circling those that looked promising. It's still a good way to look for a job.

The newspaper is still the best single source for public jobs in the geographic area served by that paper. If you are in a field that has few prospects in your local area, you will need to look in professional or trade journals that advertise jobs nationally or internationally. Remember, reading and responding to an ad is the easiest way to find a prospective position. But, it also subjects you to the most competition.

Internet Ads

With the advent of the Internet, access to the job clearing-house was made exponentially easier! The big, national bulletin boards, such as Monster or Yahoo, feature thousands of well classified jobs. The problem is you must look at many job boards, since some companies list on only one of them. There are also local job boards in every city. I live in Dallas, and there are more than 100 Internet sites for jobs in the Dallas area. It would take quite a while to click through each of them. And, when you do, you are likely to find a great deal of duplication!

Actually, this has been good for the local newspaper, because if a company would like to have complete exposure to as many qualified candidates as possible, there is only one major paper in town. There are hundreds of Internet boards, and they know job applicants are aware of this fact. The newspaper is the one place in town where **everyone** checks for ads!

In addition to job boards, most company websites also have links to job listings within their own company. All you have to do is click on the appropriate icon, and you can immediately apply for a job.

The problem with Internet postings is the amount of competition. Candidates tell me everyday when they apply online, they rarely hear from any company other than a canned auto response, generated when you click the "send" button. As far as hearing from a real person, that rarely happens due to the enormous response generated by Internet ads and postings.

Let's face it: the Internet just makes it too easy! All you have to do is click a few icons and fill out a few fields of information. In some cases, you can attach your resume, which is pretty easy. In other cases, you simply "copy/paste" paragraphs from your resume into their forms. Then, it's just a matter of click, click, click, and you're done. You don't have to type a formal letter. You don't have to look up an address and type an envelope. You don't even have to lick a stamp and mail the envelope. All you do is click away!

And, because it's so easy and fast, the company receives responses from myriads of unqualified applicants, who never would have gone to the trouble of filling out and mailing an application the old-fashioned way. That makes it harder for a qualified person to be seen by a company.

Do people get jobs off the Internet? Yes, they do. It does happen. But, the odds of it happening to you are not great. Go ahead and use the Internet, but don't depend on it. Try networking or the personal search method you see in chapter titled, "How Do I Go About Marketing ME?"

Personal Search Methods

Personal search methods encompass such processes as going to companies to apply in person, telephone calls and mail correspondence. Using these methods, you must actually do some research and find companies to which you can apply. This requires some digging, but greatly reduces the competition you will face as compared with responses to advertised and posted jobs.

Search and Employment Agencies

A search firm is different than an employment agency. There is a very simple distinction between the two. A search firm is paid by the employer. An employment agency is paid by the job seeker.

There are two kinds of search firms:

- Retained Search Firms
- Contingency Search Firms

Retained firms charge a fee which is payable whether or not a candidate is found. They are being paid to search and find candidates. These are usually exclusive searches where the job order is given to only one firm. Less than 10 percent of searches are conducted this way.

Contingency Search Firms are paid only when they successfully place a candidate in a position. Sometimes, the agency will have an exclusive right to the search. In other cases, companies may contact several contingency firms in hopes one of them will come up with a candidate.

Search firms charge big fees, and companies will use them only when other means have failed to produce qualified candidates. For example, when the company wants to insure that only qualified candidates will be presented, or when they want the search conducted in a very confidential manner, will this take place.

For new college graduates, search and employment agencies are rarely a good idea. You should not use an employment agency because of the great cost, and because you can do the same thing those agencies do—even more effectively—if you know how! And, in a later chapter, I will tell you how.

A company will pay a search fee only when they require a candidate with very specific experience. It is well worth their money to pay a fee, even a very big fee, for a candidate with the background and experience needed for a key job. A search firm must present a candidate who is fully qualified, who can "hit the ground running" the first day with little training or orientation, or who can bring experience the company does not have on its own staff. In many cases, a recruited candidate will bring new customers to the company—people he has dealt with in the past. Additionally, if the candidate comes from a competitor, he can bring knowledge of the competitor's products, methods, and customers. This kind of information is worth every bit of the search fee.

Unfortunately, new graduates rarely have this kind of track record. Therefore, a company is not willing to pay a fee for an entry-level person who must be trained to do a job. So, if you do not have a track record in your field, don't even bother calling a search agency.

Job Fairs

There is no faster way to appear before many potential employers than to attend a job fair. Most colleges sponsor job fairs where employers are invited to set up booths or tables. In times when employment is plentiful, these job fairs will feature many potential employers. In the leaner years, participation in job fairs will be much smaller.

Even if you no longer live in the city where you attended college, there will be job fairs sponsored by colleges in the community where you live. Most of the time, you may attend these events. In a few cases, colleges may check IDs at the door, but in most cases, they do not.

In addition to college sponsored job fairs, there are many public job fairs. You will find them listed in the business section of your local newspaper, the Internet, or in trade journals. As job fairs will not be listed every week in your local paper, call the paper and ask for the business editor. He will be happy to help you locate job fairs.

When you go to a job fair, dress appropriately. Wear a suit or proper business attire. Present yourself as if you were going to a job interview. For, in a true sense, you are going to an interview. However, it will be an opportunity to interview with many companies at the same time. Be sure to exchange business cards with everyone you meet. If possible, meet more than one person at each company's exhibit. When you meet someone at a job fair, you will have an open opportunity to contact that person on the phone without having to go through the interminable "cold call" screening. After all, you will be calling someone you know. Also, take resumes and present them at the career fair.

Industry Trade Shows: An Even Better Option

Another place to make multiple contacts in a day is an industry trade show. If you know the industry in which you want to work, contact the industry association and find the time and location of their trade show. The easiest way to locate a trade association is to go to any college or public library. The librarian will be able to assist you with such information. You can also look on the Internet for trade associations.

For example, if you are a chemical engineer and know you want to work in the oil industry, your local librarian will direct you to a publication, such as the Oil and Gas Journal. You can contact the journal staff and learn the specifics about a show. If you want to work in the publishing industry, contact any publisher to find the name of their trade association. Likewise, you can go to their website or, better yet, call them directly and get the information on their next event. Most trade shows are not free. However, if you are a student or new graduate, they usually will have a special reduced rate that applies to you. Call and inquire.

If you go to a convention that has a trade show, the best way to make contacts is in the exhibit hall. There, companies who are selling to the industry will have representatives waiting to talk with you.

Advantages of Trade Shows over Job Fairs

A trade show can be more valuable than a job fair for the following reasons:

- Less competition—most attendees are not there looking for jobs
- Direct contact with hiring officials—you will be more likely to speak with officers of the company and department heads, who have direct hiring authority, whereas, at job fairs, you will most likely be talking to personnel managers
- Greater exposure to the industry—there will be a much larger participation from companies at trade shows than at job fairs, where only a few companies might be represented
- Better exposure to companies—because you were clever enough to think of this option, companies will be impressed with your ability to make things happen

Personal Search Methods

In the chapter on networking, we discussed how you can make contact with numerous people, starting with those you already know. This method often will lead you to someone who might offer you a position. Personal search methods differ from networking in that you do not necessarily start with people you know. Through this method, you find the names of people in the job field of your choice, approach those people and present yourself for a job.

We mentioned earlier that employment agencies (the kind where you pay a fee) do certain things to find a job for you. You can do the same thing for yourself, and it won't cost you any money. However, it will require a great commitment of time and effort.

Just what does an employment agency do when they search for a job for you? The first thing they try to do is match you up with a job order that has been submitted by one of their client companies. Only on rare occasion does this produce a job possibility for you. If they cannot match you up, they will put you in their database and, hopefully, in the future, the computer will identify a job match for you. But don't hold your breath. The next thing they might do is try to "market" you to companies they know in your field that hire people like you. How do they do this? It's very simple. They develop a list of companies. They develop a list of contacts in those companies. Then, they get on the telephone and call, call, call. Hopefully, they will come across someone who is interested in your background.

There are some real problems with this approach as pertains to you, however. The first problem is companies would rather hear from you directly, than through an agent. They want someone who has the tenacity to work hard looking for a job, not someone who is relying on others to do it for him. This is particularly true as it applies to new graduates. When you become an experienced professional, this will no longer be the case. If you have a skill that is hard to find and have special abilities to offer, they will send a search firm to seek you out. In that case, they will appreciate you more if they have to pay a fee. But, as a new person starting out, you will do better finding a job on your own.

The second problem with an employment agency is it is highly improbable they will select you as a candidate to market. A typical agency has hundreds of candidates. Marketing a candidate to a long list of companies is a time consuming process, and one of their agents can market only one person a day. In selecting the one person to present, they will choose the one they feel they can most easily place. If you are not that person, your application will die and be buried in their vast file cabinet. Only if their computer search happens to turn up a matching opportunity will you ever hear from them. So, the key: market yourself to companies.

Pursuing a Company Rather Than a Job

Most of the time, your job search will center on a job interest. For example, if you are seeking a job as a chemical engineer, you will make a list of chemical companies and seek a job with one of those companies.

In other cases, you might want to focus on a particular company, which may have jobs that would be suitable for you. I recently asked a client how he found his first career job. He told me his father had worked for Ford Motor Company, and through his dad's contacts, he was able to land a summer job at Ford. Knowing there were hundreds of opportunities for chemical engineers at Ford, he accepted the first one that became available. After about a year, he found he was interested in the paint side of the business and decided to move his career in that direction.

This is a particularly good strategy under certain circumstances:

- If you have a specific geographic preference
- If you have a general education, but no specific job preference as yet
- If you have relatives or friends who work for a certain company
- If your desire to work for a large company is stronger than your desire for a specific job
- If you seek a management position that could be accessed from several career paths within the company

Let me expand briefly on some of these options.

I obtained my first job through a personal job search. Through the hospital association, I developed a list of every hospital in Texas over a certain size. I then contacted the administrators. I contacted about 60 hospitals. The responses came in, and the list narrowed to about three. Eventually, I received and accepted the offer from Ft. Worth.

I found my job with a geographic preference of the state of Texas, which gave me many choices. As a young, single person in Ft. Worth, I had many friends who were born and raised in that city and wanted to go to work there. That meant a young person with a business degree, who wanted to work for a large company in Ft. Worth, had only a few choices, as Ft. Worth did not have many huge corporations in 1970. They had a choice of about 20 companies.

The largest employer in the city was General Dynamics, a huge defense contractor. They employed 35,000 people at their peak. Many of my friends had family members who worked there. One had a degree in electrical engineering. He wanted to work in that field, but had no preference whether he designed advanced radar systems, guidance systems, antenna systems, or any other kind of electrical engineering. system. He simply wanted to work for that company in his career field. Therefore, he directed his job search toward General Dynamics. With so many employees, it was certain they would have a job for a person like him. His challenge was to break into the system.

Another friend had a business degree. She didn't care whether she worked in the Defense Contract Administration area, the accounting department, the purchasing department, or any other department. She simply wanted to find one of the 35,000 jobs that were available for people with business degrees.

I had another friend who wanted to be a department store manager. There were six major department stores in the city, three of which were local. Therefore, this young man centered his job search on those three stores, knowing it would not be hard to find a general position with one of those companies, if he were willing to start at the bottom and work his way up. And, it didn't matter whether he started in the toy department, the shipping department or any other department, since his goal was to become a store manager. He could become a part of their management training starting in any of those areas.

The best example of a person wanting to work for a large organization is, of course, the military. I have a college friend who joined the Army after college. He didn't care whether he served in the Infantry, the Artillery, or any other branch of the Army. His goal in life was not to fire a certain kind of weapon. He wanted to rise in the ranks. He wanted to become a commander, and he did just that He ended his career as a three star general. The major point here is he wanted to be in the Army.

Chapter 15

Internships: How Can I Learn My Way Into a Job?

Another excellent way for a new or recent graduate to enter a preferred job is to take an internship. It's much easier than finding a permanent job, and it allows you to "taste before you buy." Internships come in three varieties:

1. Formal Internships
2. Management Training Programs
3. Temporary Positions

The Temporary Agency Approach

Another personal job search method is the Temporary Agency approach. Many companies use temporary agencies as their primary strategy for filling certain positions. The strength of this approach is it gives both the company and the employee the opportunity to taste before you buy. When you sign up with an agency for a temporary position related to your job objective, you place yourself in an excellent position to find a permanent job. Here are some advantages:

- It's easy to sign up and register with a temporary agency.
- You have the opportunity to get to know people in many different companies.
- You can get inside specific companies you would like to work for, and make contacts you could never make from the outside.

- It places you in an excellent position to network with people while on the temporary job, especially in companies that may not have permanent jobs.
- You can try out different kinds of jobs.
- You can try out different types of companies—large or small, public or private.
- You can gain valuable experience that will enhance your knowledge, your skills, your resume, and, hence, your value to other prospective employers.

There are several types of temporary agencies that contract for different kinds of jobs. Here's a list of the types of agencies found in the ATT Yellow Pages listings for Dallas, Texas as well as the number of·agencies in each category:

- Accountants Employment Agencies (13)
- Administrative Assistants Employment Agencies (12)
- Advertising Employment Agencies (3)
- Chefs Employment Agencies (2)
- Clerical Employment Agencies (11)
- Computer Marketing Employment Agencies (3)
- Computer Programmers Employment Agencies (3)
- Computer Technical Support Employment Agencies (3)
- Data Processing Employment Agencies (2)
- Desktop Publishing Employment Agencies(1)
- Disability Employment Agencies (1)
- Domestic Help Employment Agencies (40)
- Drafting Employment Agencies (2)
- Employment Information (1)
- Engineers Employment Agencies (4)
- Executives Employment Agencies (10)
- Factory Labor Employment Agencies (5)
- Financial Analysts Employment Agencies (5)

- High Tech Employment Agencies (14)
- Hotel & Motel Employment Agencies (2)
- Human Resource Consultants Employment Agencies (6)
- Insurance Employment Agencies (4)
- Legal Secretaries Employment Agencies (4)
- Medical Personnel Employment Agencies (8)
- Paralegal Employment Agencies (2)
- Restaurant Employment Agencies (1)
- Sales Employment Agencies (7)
- Secretarial Employment Agencies (3)
- Temporary Employment Agencies (365)
- Word Processing Employment Agencies (1)

There's a temporary employment agency for almost every kind of work you can imagine! You can use experience gained in temporary jobs to qualify you for the job you eventually want to land.

For example, suppose you have a business degree and a great interest in factory management but have little or no actual factory management experience. You can sign up with an agency that handles "factory labor employment." You will have the opportunity to experience many kinds of jobs in factory situations. You can spend as much or as little time as you wish on any kind of job. You will have the opportunity to rub shoulders with plant managers, network with them and learn from them. Also, when you are a "temp," you can enjoy a different kind of relationship with the management, since you are not directly in the chain of command. If you play your cards right, they will train you and give you the experience to find the job you desire.

Internships

I want to start this part of the book with what I think is a dramatic example from my own experience. When I was only 22 years of age, I started my first job out of college as "second in command" of a 400-bed hospital with 1,200 employees. Just think. When my boss was out of town, and a decision had to be made, the buck stopped with me! How could I have obtained such a lofty position at a young age? The answer: I served a one-year internship, which was part of my master's degree program in hospital administration! That was the ticket that earned such a high position for such an inexperienced person. Even I admit this internship had far more weight than it should have carried. But, that's what an internship can do for you!

Internships are one of the oldest ways to execute job training. The have worn many different names throughout the centuries. Interns have been called residents, apprentices, novices, trainees, beginners, grunts, shavetails, and a host of other names. Internships are "on the job training programs," as opposed to academic programs.

The term, "intern," until about 30 years ago, usually referred to physicians-in-training. Since then, the term has quickly gained popular use in virtually every other field. Some internships are paid; some are unpaid; some are performed in undergraduate situations; others are for graduates; some internships are formally structured programs, while others are merely situations where interns walk in the footsteps of their preceptors.

In many cases, an internship is the necessary ticket to gain entrance into a profession. I spoke with a young person who was looking for a position in an advertising agency. She told me these positions are so highly sought, in order to obtain a position in a significant firm, you must serve as an unpaid intern before you can get your foot in the door.

My son obtained a paid internship that turned into a part time job, which, in turn, became a full time position. My niece recently served a paid internship with one of the major political parties and worked full time on a senatorial campaign. Their internships were real world experiences, which could never be fully simulated in university settings.

Finding Internships

To find internships, go to your college's career services office and to the department office of your major department. Also, simply type the word, "internships" into any search engine on the Internet, and you will find thousands of available opportunities.

Not all internships will open the door as dramatically as mine did for me, but a good internship under a seasoned professional can jumpstart your career in impressive fashion. Also, if you serve that internship under the aegis and supervision of the right person, that person can become a mentor and have the influence and power to open the doors of success in any profession, not only as you begin your career, but also in decades to come.

Management Training Programs

Although they are not called internships, management training programs serve the same purposes. The main difference is an internship usually follows a defined time period, and neither the company nor the intern has any commitment beyond the internship.

As a management trainee, you have already become a regular employee, though you will probably be doing the same things an intern does. As such, the company is making an investment in you. And, it goes without saying—they do not want to lose their investment! Training a new person is quite costly, and the company wants a return from their investment of time, money, and effort.

When I worked as a package boy for a grocery store in my initial employment, they selected good workers, who desired a career in the grocery business and placed them in their management training program. Some went on to become department managers, assistant managers, store managers and corporate executives from that humble beginning in the management training program.

The moral to this section is even if you don't obtain a formal internship, your entry-level or menial job can become the equivalent of an internship if you work with management and let them know of your intent to learn and move up.

Chapter 16

How Do I Go About Marketing ME?

How to Market Yourself to Companies

How do people usually go about marketing themselves to companies? Let me start with a personal example. About 25 years ago, when I was in hospital administration, one day, the Board of Directors went into executive session and emerged to announce my boss and I were out! I found myself on the street pounding the pavement looking for a job. So, what did I do?

I knew, at that point, I wanted to make a career change. I thought I might market my background in health care administration to find a job in the claims administration area of the insurance industry. I made a list of three companies. I thought I might just pay them a visit and try to make a contact in person. I visited the first company and received nothing but their good wishes. I visited the second and third companies with the same results. I spent a day-and-a-half in that endeavor. I was completely discouraged! I thought no one wanted me! What was I to do?

The problem was I was limiting my search to only a few companies. You must consider the odds for any search: there is only a 1 percent chance any company will need someone like you at any given time. All that means is in order to find a job in a general search, when there are no personal connections, you must contact 100 companies for the odds to work in your favor. In networking, the key to success is face to face contact. In a personal marketing search, the key to making that contact is **the telephone.** That's right! The telephone, not personal visits or the computer, is the essential tool.

Let me say one word of warning about the computer. It has become a comfort zone for job searchers, especially young job searchers, such as recent college graduates. It's most tempting for them to sit behind the computer and click away at job boards and company sites, thinking they are doing everything possible to find a job. Jobs are won through personal contact, and the computer removes job searchers one step further from the people who can act to give them a job.

The Plan

In order to avoid the discouragement that comes from rejection, you need to make 100 calls at once! You need to realize the odds are that each company will say, "Thanks, but no thanks." If you make 100 calls, you should expect 95 "no's," five "maybe's" and, perhaps, two offers after all is said and done.

You may say, "Hey, wait a minute, isn't that being rather negative—expecting a 95 percent response of "no's." Shouldn't my attitude be just the opposite—expecting a 95 percent positive response?" The answer is: I'm being realistic. This particular job search strategy is not necessarily an easy one. It is effective only if hearing "no" does not frustrate you. With this plan, you're going to hear negative answers. You should simply expect them and move on until you hear those few "yes's." A successful baseball player gets put out three times for every time he gets a hit. He's not going to enjoy success unless he's willing to put up with the failures. Babe Ruth struck out more than other players. He knew he wasn't going to hit home runs unless he swung hard enough. And, when he swung that hard, he often missed the ball altogether. But, he connected enough to make him "the king."

Step One: Select a Job Title

The first thing you need to do in marketing yourself is select the specific job you want to do. Hopefully, you have already gone through the steps to identify potential job titles you think would be best for you. That is, you know the job you want to apply for!

The Company Marketing List

For the purpose of marketing yourself to companies, you need to develop a list—a calling list for this purpose. This is a simple, four-column list with four headings:

1. Company Name
2. Company Contact (the person to call)
3. Telephone Number
4. Results of Call

Before you make the first marketing call, however, it is important to list the 100 target companies, the company contacts for each of those companies, and the phone numbers of those contacts BEFORE you make the first call.

Step Two: Identify Potential Employers

General job, no industry preference, specific location

The second step in marketing yourself is to develop a list of
companies that hire people like you. There are several ways
to do this. If you have an occupation that is broad and
general, the list should not be hard to generate. If you have a
specific place you want to live, you should select a mix of
large and small companies.

For example, if you have credentials in accounting,
purchasing, sales, or any other occupation, and if you do not
have a particular preference, then you should select a variety
of companies in various industries or professions. Your list
should include both large and small companies. You should
develop a list of 100 potential employers.

Specific job, specific industry, specific location

If you have a very specific job that requires a certain
industry, it is much easier to identify potential employers.
For example, if you have a degree in medical technology,
physical therapy or one of the health professions, you will
develop a list of hospitals, both large and small. Additionally,
there are clinics and independent labs that hire people like
you. They should be included, also.

If you have a degree in mechanical engineering and have a
location preference in a large industrial area, it should not be
difficult to develop a list of 100 companies.

If you have a specific job with limited employers in your preferred area, developing the list may be more of a challenge. Here are some resources that can help you:

- Business References (Thomas Register, Dun & Bradstreet, Standard & Poors)
- Internet Search Engines
- College Career Services
- Professional Association Directories
- Public Library
- Chamber of Commerce
- Yellow Pages

If you are not in the same community as your college, take advantage of the resources of the public library. The librarian is one of the most valuable consultants you will ever meet. In this Internet generation when so much information is available online, many young people are not accustomed to working with librarians and don't realize how much assistance they can give. Best of all, their services are free! Maybe that's why many people don't take advantage of their expertise. And, last but not least, consider the Yellow Pages. Companies within a locale are all listed by category. There you will find many potential employers you may never learn of any other way.

Government jobs

If you are interested in government jobs, there are several websites that specialize in government positions of all kinds. Again, your college career service or your librarian can help identify potential agencies at the federal, state and local levels. You must apply for specific government jobs. In most jurisdictions, you must apply individually in each agency.

Remember, the timeline for government jobs can be a
lengthy one.

Political Connections

If you are seeking a government position, enough could
never be said about political connections. A public official at
any level of government can be very helpful in opening the
right doors for you.

During the Great Depression in 1930, my father found
himself unable to earn a living. He was a doctor, one year out
of medical school. He tried to start a medical practice in a
small town, but people had no money to pay their bills. My
mother's father was a well-known and well-connected
businessman in Kansas City, Missouri. At that time, city
employment was almost impossible to find. But, my
grandfather knew one of the county judges in Kansas City
and arranged for my dad to go his office. One of the judges
was none other than Harry S. Truman, who would later
become the 33rd President of the United States. This contact
paved the way for him to obtain work from the city.

As time progressed, another political connection proved
valuable. Because my grandfather knew one of the senators
from Missouri, another meeting was arranged, and my father
obtained a job in the Missouri State Hospital system.
Actually, no job was available at the time, but because of the
political connection, one was created.

As a young graduate, you may feel some reluctance to use
connections to advance your career over others who do not
have those contacts. If that is the case, let me say that you
will soon learn that connections are "what make the world go
'round."

Step Three: Identify Contacts in Those Companies

This is possibly the most difficult step in the entire process. Remember one very important point: the purpose of this step is NOT to talk to the person at the company. The purpose is ONLY to get the name of the best possible person to talk to about a job! When you call a company, for whom do you ask when seeking a job? Do you ask for the Human Resources Department? Do you ask for the department head? Do you ask for the CEO? Do you ask for the owner? The answer is you could speak with any of the above. Whom you call depends upon several factors including:

- The nature of the job
- The size of the company
- Your ability to access the desired person

Concerning that third factor, your ability to access the desired person, you may not be able to find the name of a department head in the company. Even if he is the desired person, it may be necessary to accept the name of the personnel manager or recruiting manager.

As a general rule, you want to find the name of the department manager of the appropriate department first. That should be your objective. In a very small company, you will want to speak with the owner or general manager. In a medium-sized company, you may even ask for the CEO or president or vice president. Even if he or she refers you to someone else, you can at least say you were referred by the higher person. If you cannot obtain any other name, it's ok to speak with the human resources manager or someone in that area.

Recall the section on cold call networking. I told you how to find names of people to call for networking purposes.

What are some other ways of finding the name of the person you want to speak with? Here are some more suggestions:

- Obtain the name from a corporate directory
- Obtain the name from the company's Web page
- Obtain the name from a professional association directory
- Call the company and ask the receptionist, operator, or whoever answers
- Call the company and ask for another person who might be more likely to give you the information

The problem with obtaining the name from a corporate directory such as Dun & Bradstreet or a library listing is, quite often, only top corporate officers are listed. You are unlikely to find the name of a department manager in the department to which you need to apply. The same is true with the company's Web page. However, this is not always the case, and it is always worth a try to search the Web page for such information.

Let me illustrate. Suppose you have a degree in accounting and wish to talk with the controller of the company. This may not be listed in a corporate directory; however, the vice president for finance may be listed. It's okay to call this person, though it is unlikely you will make contact. The receptionist who answers, however, will likely give you the name of the controller. Another approach is simply to call the main number of the company and ask the receptionist, "Who is the controller of the company?" There is a 50/50 chance that person will give you the name without hassle. You see, receptionists or operators, especially in large companies, are trained to screen calls and direct people like job seekers to a personnel department number. There, you may well be greeted with a prerecorded answering device that will direct you to the company Web page. That's exactly where you DON'T want to go!

Still another approach is to call the company and ask for the Accounts Receivable or the Accounts Payable department. This department is publicly accessible because they want to talk to people who want to pay their bills! You will be connected! Then, you can ask the person who answers for the name of the controller. Most likely, the accounts receivable clerk will give you that name. He is NOT trained or assigned to screen or redirect calls.

And, let me repeat. At this stage, you only want to obtain a name. You DO NOT yet want to make your personal marketing call. When you get the name, say, "Thank you very much" and end the phone call.

What if that doesn't work or if you want to speak with some department that does not have public accessibility? You can then ask for the mail room or the receiving dock (in the case of a manufacturing company) or some other department that does have a public outlet.

Getting In Through the "Back Door!"

Call the company after hours and listen to the recording. Often, it will supply department extensions, which you can access directly the following day. Or, you can place a random call, as explained in a previous chapter, and request information from whoever answers. If you tell the person why you are calling and request the name of a department head, he will probably help you. If not, try another random call. (This takes guts, but it pays dividends).

There's one more thing you can do when you call total strangers in the company. If you have good conversations, keep their names in your networking file. You may have occasion to call them back. They will remember you because they rarely receive such unexpected calls from total strangers.

Again, if you are not given the name of the department head or hiring authority, ask for the name of the personnel manager.

Another approach is to call the office of the CEO and talk to whoever answers the phone. Unlike the receptionists who answer the main line, you will find the assistant or secretary to the CEO to be a most cordial and most helpful person. (That's why they hired such a person for the position)! While the assistant probably will not connect you with the "big boss," he will direct you by name to the person you need. You can then tell that individual you were referred by the boss's assistant. In fact, you should ask the assistant for his or her name, so you can "name drop" when you make your marketing call. Believe me, such an approach will make a BIG DIFFERENCE.

When you get the name of the hiring authority with whom you wish to speak, write it down next to the company name! Finding 100 names for the 100 companies will be a tedious task, but you should take the time to do it. Doing it the right way will pay dividends in the end.

Step 4: Obtain the Direct Phone Numbers

On your four column list, write the direct dial number of the person you want to call. The specific number may be different than the main number of the company. Go to the trouble to obtain the direct number. It will save time and make the calling process smoother, easier and faster.

Step 5: Prepare for Your Personal Marketing Campaign

The key to receiving positive results from your personal marketing calls is to make proper preparation and to make an appeal. You should:

1. Write your marketing script
2. Practice your marketing script

Maybe you've never used a script before. You've probably heard such hideous examples of calling scripts from telemarketers that you're appalled at the thought. Let me assure you, as I related in a previous chapter, there's nothing amateur or "Mickey Mouse" about using a script. The only downside would be to use it in an unpracticed or clumsy manner.

Making an Appeal For Help

About three years ago, my family and I were on vacation in Europe. Our experienced traveler friends told me I didn't need to make hotel reservations that time of year, since it was before the big rush of tourists. Our family showed up in Florence, Italy, about 10 p.m. I went to a hotel to check in and found they were full. No problem! I went to the hotel next door. Full! I journeyed on to a couple of others. The clerk told me I would not find a vacancy in Florence that night and sent me to another town. Guess what? No vacancy. On to the next town—same problem. Finally at 1:00 a.m., after a series of rejections, I decided to make an **appeal** to the desk clerk. As tired and weary as we were, there was no question about my desperation! I passionately exclaimed to the clerk, "It's one o'clock in the morning. I've been looking for a room for three hours and nobody has a place for us. If we don't find a room soon, we'll have to sleep in the car. Won't you please help me find a room?" The clerk got on the phone, made several calls, and found me a room. It was 40 minutes away, but he produced results for me. Why? Because **I made an appeal!**

You say, "Who do you think I am? I'm not going to beg someone for a job." I'm not asking you to beg. I'm saying if you don't want to be referred to the usual channels, you must say something different than the ordinary bloke. And, if you've gone to the trouble of preparing a calling sheet, as I've described (which requires much effort), then you'd better have something to say that will get their attention. An appeal will do this!

The script should have three points:

- Who You Are
- Why You're Calling
- An Appeal for Consideration

Here's an example:

"Hello, Mr. Smith, my name is Fred Cooper. I'm a recent college graduate trying to find my first career position. I'm running into all the usual roadblocks, and, as you know, the doors are being closed before I even get to step in. I understand you are the manager of the accounting division, and so I'm making an appeal to see if you have a position available where I might be considered.

If you get the anticipated "no," turn it into a networking call. Also, even though there is no job opening, you should ask if you could send a resume.

On the other hand, if there is an opening, and he says, "yes, tell me more," be prepared to give your 30-second presentation. Notice the three points:

- Who You Are: a recent graduate looking for an entry-level position
- Why You're Calling: the personnel department has given you the run around and won't even let you in the door
- An Appeal for Consideration: therefore, I found you and am coming directly to you

This is just one example. You may have a better and more creative script. Write your script and practice it with several friends. See what they think!

Step 6: Do It!

After you decide on the script, you're ready to start making your calls. The first five calls will be the most difficult. You'll be breaking the ice. Remember, you have everything written down on your page:

1. The name of the company
2. The name of the best contact you could find
3. The phone number

The fourth column should feature the results of the call.

Okay, enough procrastinating! Do it! Make that first call! They'll probably tell you some form of "no!" They may refer you to personnel. They may tell you they're not hiring. They may tell you that you've called the wrong person. Whatever they tell you, write it down in the results column. Keep a good record of your calls.

You should expect to hear a "no," and it should come as no surprise. But, remember, you will also hear an occasional form of "yes." They may tell you to send a resume. They may refer you to someone else in the company. They may even ask you to come in. Listen for this kind of response and follow-up appropriately.

Make a note in your results column and put a big red asterisk by it. If they ask you to send a resume, allow enough time for them to receive and review it, then place a follow-up phone call. Your objective—at this stage—is a face to face interview.

Your overall objective from the 100 calls should be five positive responses that could turn into interviews. If you achieve this goal, you will have been very successful.

Chapter 17

Who Will Help Me Get the Job
And
Who Will Help Me Get Going in the Job?

As you market yourself to find the job of your dreams, you will need some help. You will also need guidance as you start your career. Here is some advice regarding people who can give you the help you need.

A Good Mentor: The Key to Success in Your Career

When I started my career in the hospital business, a friend and fraternity brother of mine started work at a different hospital. For the first few years, our careers were somewhat parallel. Though we both had high-sounding positions and impressive titles, we had little actual power and authority. You see, we both served under dominant bosses, who micromanaged everything we did. We were the same in many ways. In other ways, we were different. (As I have mentioned earlier, I really was not well-suited to be a manager, while he definitely was). But, in addition, he had one extremely important and necessary advantage I did not have: **he had a mentor.**

His boss was an older man, a well-known, highly esteemed leader in hospital administration. My boss, on the other hand, was a young man, an unknown entity in the profession. Moreover, he was considered to be somewhat of a maverick or renegade in the political circles of the hospital association.

Unfortunately for me, it was not to my advantage for career growth purposes to be associated with him.

More importantly, because my boss was young and not well established, he considered me to be more of a rival than an understudy, and he was not disposed to helping me grow in the profession. Indeed, he considered the assistants under him to be potential usurpers of his position and power. For this reason, he did more to hold us down than lift us up.

Of the five or six assistants who served under that first boss, only one really grew in the profession. In fact, most of us left the field after a few years. My friend, who had the mentor, is now CEO of one of the largest healthcare systems in the nation and one of the most powerful figures in American healthcare today.

What Is A Mentor?

Mentors are father or mother-like figures, who consider you to be their protégés, and take it upon themselves to make you successful. They guide you through the minefields and pitfalls of organizational life. They chuckle at your youthful blunders. They teach you, train you, discipline you, advise you, cajole you, and encourage you. They lift you up when you fall and protect you from the wolves, which would otherwise devour you if left to your own devices. They use their influences to pave the way for your success as you mature and prove yourself ready for major responsibility.

Many years ago, I heard a management speaker who said if you did not have a mentor when you started your career, the likelihood of success would be difficult and greatly diminished. The longer I live, the more I observe such to be true.

Finding a Mentor

If it is true you need a mentor, then one of your great challenges is to find that mentor. As you interview for jobs, you may be fortunate to land a mentor by chance. However, this possibility is unlikely for most people.

Remember, a mentor, above all else, is a person who likes you an awful lot! His interest goes far beyond business. It's personal! Maybe you are potentially the "son" or "daughter" he never had! Maybe, he looks at you and sees himself when he was your age. A mentor is a person whose heart interest is greater than his head interest. He will take you on as the special project in his life. He will go to bat for you. He will place his own reputation on the line, as he promotes you and your career.

If you could discover a mentor before you take a job, it would be nice, but it's unlikely! If you obtain your job through networking, you may be able to recognize the potential in advance. In fact, that's the very reason a networking contact may hire you for a job that didn't exist when you were there. He wants to be your mentor and develop your career.

If you go to work for a family-owned company with family members in line to take control, the "kids coming up" are the ones most likely to be mentored. However, senior members in the family are also on the lookout for loyal nonfamily members who will support the efforts of the family. They may take you on as a mentor for this reason.

I know a young man who received a job in a governor's office as political payback to his family. It was a great job, but it was up to him whether he would be handled as a protégé or a burden to be tolerated. It's sort of like the boss's nephew who is hired because of family pressure. The nephew can become a hated pest or a valued protégé. It's totally up to him, and the way he handles the situation.

Finding a mentor is something you have to do on your own. If you can develop the possibility before you get the job—Great! Most likely, you will have to do that after you get there. Let me add, it's possible, even in a huge organization.

The best example I know is the military. When you join the Army, you have no idea for whom you will work, nor can it be prearranged, unless perhaps, you are the son or daughter of a four star general! If you enter as an officer, you will be just another one of the young lieutenants, unless you take steps to find a mentor.

How do you do something about it? How do you find a mentor? He will, most likely, be old enough to be your father. He will be someone who is, today, where you want to be, tomorrow. He will be the "old man," the colonel who has taken a liking to you for some personal reason. Maybe you'll be acquainted with him through church or the golf course. Maybe you'll work under him. Maybe he thinks you would be the right person for his son or daughter. Maybe he just likes the way you look, or the way you talk, or the way you do your work, so he wants to take a special interest in you.

The key is to latch on to such a person. Ask his advice. Go to him with the challenges you face and seek his counsel. Place yourself under his authority and give him the honor he deserves. Ask him to help you. You'll be able to tell he if wants to take you under his wing. When that relationship happens, don't take it for granted. Follow his counsel. Trust him. Do what he says. He's been in your place before you, and knows his way in the business. If you do walk with your mentor in a proper way, he will not only tell you and show you how to do things, he will make those things happen for you!

We would like to think we could pull ourselves up by our bootstraps. We would like to think we need no one to get ahead. If you'll look at the people who progress, I think you'll find that 90 percent of them had some significant help along the way from someone higher on the food chain. And there's absolutely nothing wrong with taking advantage of such assistance. In fact, anyone who has the opportunity and neglects the offer is foolish.

A word of warning: there is a difference between finding a true mentor and a political ally. A political ally can open doors for you. The difference is the political ally has, first and foremost, his own interests in mind. A mentor has your interests in mind! The political guy will help you for a short season; a mentor will help you for a lifetime.

Politics and the Job Search

When I was a young boy, we played a game called "King of the Mountain." In this game, we would assemble on a small hill or a large sand pile. The object of the game was to ascend to the top of the hill and occupy that position. The boys (in those days, girls did not play those kinds of games) would try to wrestle and fight their way to the top, and depose the one who occupied the exalted position. Several strategies were employed. The biggest, strongest guys, of course, had an advantage. Other boys would form little alliances to knock a stronger boy to a lower level. Eventually, a smarter kid would use his head and people skills to get others to do his dirty work, and he would ultimately end up on top of the heap!

It was a little kid's version of one of those popular reality TV shows you see today—shows like, "Survivor," "The Apprentice" or "The Bachelor." Of course, there are myriads of games people play that have a similar objective.

Politics is a part of life—a part of every aspect of life. We would like to think this is not true, but it is. Politics is, simply stated, the struggle for power and dominance, the contest to determine who will rule. I punched in the term on dictionary.com and found this definition, "Intrigue or maneuvering within a political unit or group in order to gain control or power."

You find politics in families, businesses, churches, schools, clubs, sports teams and every kind of group that exists. Yes, you even find it in government!

You will also discover politics will figure into your search for your first job. Politics can be clean or dirty, but it's always there. Everyone who rises to any place of power or authority has used one form of politics or another.

Consider the men who have been President of the United States. When you think of word politics, that's the ultimate prize in this country. Some have risen from humble places. Others have risen out of "American nobility." This principle applies to both parties. Republicans have their Bush's and their Reagan's. Democrats have their Kennedy's and their Clintons. The key is each man started with the hand he was dealt and made the best of it.

That's what you must do as you select your career and find your first position. You need to identify your natural strengths and weaknesses. Hopefully, you have already taken stock of yourself and done this.

Politics works in the job search process by finding and harnessing the help you need to land the job you want! In the chapter on networking, we discussed your personal circle of contacts, and how the people you know could help you in making networking contacts. Your network may also be able to help you as you pursue more standard job search methods. There are two ways they can help—introductions and references.

When you approach a company and you know no one, you are a stranger as far as they are concerned. And, companies do practice the principle that you should be wary of strangers. At the point you meet, you are a "cold contact." However, if you know even one person on the hiring chain, your status changes drastically for the better. If you have a friend in common, you become a "warm contact." Unfortunately, the opposite is also true. If you have a "nonfriend," you're probably toast!

If you are applying to a company where a friend or relative works, you start the game way ahead, since people always want to hire someone about whom they know something good.

In some cases, your contact can simply introduce you to a company, even if no references are involved. Just the mention of the fact they know who you are, will open doors for you. This is particularly true of contacts, such as fraternity or alumni.

If you want to work as an engineer for the Texas Highway Department and you say you graduated from Texas A&M University, this alone will move you to the front of the line. If you are in the same fraternity or social club, politics will help you, likewise. The same applies to church affiliations, hobby preferences or even the sports teams you root for! That's the beauty of politics.

Obviously, if someone knows you well enough to give you a reference, it will make a world of difference. References from people they know carry 10 times the weight of unknown references.

Taking advantage of a political contact is quite different than benefiting from a mentor. As mentioned in the previous chapter, a mentor will help you because he has a genuine interest in you and your well-being. A political contact expects something in return. They will expect to receive a "quid pro quo" at some point in the future. Or, at least, they will anticipate a "thanks" in some way. It's certainly a good idea to return those favors.

Can political maneuvering cross over ethical lines? Certainly, so! Therefore, you must be very careful how you utilize political favors. A salesman may use his influence with a company, expecting patronage from you in the future.

To many people, politics is an ugly word and an ugly process. You may feel the use of political favors to get a job, or, at least, an opportunity for a job, is somewhat demeaning and even unprofessional. I suppose there are times when this could be the case. However, you need to be aware of "what makes the world go 'round."

Chapter 18

Summing It All Up

Finding your first job is like planting a seed. If you do it right, it will grow through each stage of development and establish a strong and fulfilling career, which, like a great tree, will produce fruit for a lifetime.

Find a job you like to do—something you want to do with your life. In some cases, practicality will dictate you do something second best. Regardless, get on a track that's right for you. You spend one-third of your waking hours at work in your lifetime. To do something you don't like will result in a life of disappointment.

In most cases, you will change careers several times. In some cases, such a change will be forced upon you. I have a cousin who went into the men's clothing business selling suits. He was in the business for many years until the clothing business went south! He then had to start the process over again and find something else.

In other cases, you will find your interests have changed, and you desire to do something else. In my case, when I left hospital administration, I pursued a different kind of work and eventually landed in the executive search and recruiting field.

Still, in other cases, you will go as far as you can in a job and must pick another career in order to progress professionally or financially. I have a friend who worked as a staff accountant for a large firm. After a number of years, he reached his peak income. If he were to progress, he realized he would have to pursue the sales aspect of the firm.

As I mentioned earlier, most people change jobs seven times in a lifetime. I'm not sure of the statistics on career changes. Perhaps you must go through the described disciplines several times. This book focuses on the strategies that apply to new graduates seeking their first jobs. There are other books that deal with strategies for people in their 30s, 40s, 50s, and yes, even for those who make changes in their 60s and beyond.

I hope this book gives you the guidance and strategies you need to chart your course and pursue it with success and satisfaction.